D1431849

"We Can Do Together"

*to Coriana
who passtim for
creative images &
having the world
in striving
Blessings
Chapman
6-14-2013*

Dagmar Braun Celeste, ca. 1978.

"We Can Do Together"

Impressions of a Recovering
Feminist First Lady

Dagmar Braun Celeste

THE KENT STATE UNIVERSITY PRESS

Kent & London

© 2002 by The Kent State University Press, Kent, Ohio 44242
All rights reserved
Library of Congress Catalog Card Number 2001002016
ISBN 0-87338-718-x
Manufactured in the United States of America

06   05   04   03   02   5   4   3   2   1

Library of Congress Cataloging-in-Publication Data
Celeste, Dagmar Braun, 1941–
We can do together : impressions of a recovering feminist first lady /
Dagmar Braun Celeste.
p.   cm.
Includes index.
ISBN 0-87338-718-x (pbk. : alk. paper) ∞
1. Celeste, Dagmar, 1941–
2. Governors' spouses—Ohio—Biography.
3. Feminists—Ohio—Biography.
4. Ohio—Politics and government—1951–
5. Celeste, Richard F.
I. Title
F496.4.C45 A3 2002
977.1'033'092—dc21   2001002016

British Library Cataloging-in-Publication data are available.

In memory of
Utzi-Dorly Braun, my sister and guardian angel,
and the numerous soul sisters and spiritual guides who have been
my faithful companions on the journey home.
And, in gratitude,
to Ohio, my home, and all her wonderful people,
past, present, and future;
to Richard F. Celeste, my one and only spouse and best mentor;
to our children, Eric, Christopher, Gabriella,
Noelle, Natalie, and Stephen;
and to our grandchildren, here already and yet to come.

Have you ever seen the sun rise in Ohio?
Have you ever seen Ohio in the fall?
The farmlands and the towns, the busy city sounds,
Seems to me Ohio has it all.

Lately I've been thinking about Ohio,
Thinking what Ohio means to me.
I am glad to have it known Ohio is my home.
I want it to be all that it can be.

And I think I can do something for Ohio.
I want to see Ohio be the best.
I care enough to care about Ohio,
So I am coming out to vote for Dick Celeste.

Do you care enough to care about Ohio?
Are you proud to say Ohio is your home?
Do you believe we can do together
all the things we can't do alone?

Contents

Foreword

by Mary E. Hess

More than ten years ago—a period of time that feels like an eon to me rather than a mere decade—I worked for Dagmar as her communications coordinator. Part of that role included coordinating her projects with the Core Circle, a diverse group of very bright and lively women from across the state of Ohio who gathered periodically to help Dagmar choose and focus her projects.

As her time as First Lady began to draw to a close, it was clear that the work of the Core Circle, both in its structure as well as its tasks, was very innovative and unique in the history of "First Lady-dom," and we tried to come up with ways to adequately describe and document the process of building this feminist policy group. One of the ideas was to help Dagmar write her personal history as a collaborative group project. Members of the Core Circle spent hours interviewing Dagmar, and then those tapes were painstakingly transcribed.

Eventually I was given the task of trying to build some order out of thousands of pages of raw transcript, to try to create an outline for a book. At the same time I was falling deeply in love with Dagmar's oldest son, Eric, and so was also being drawn more closely into the intimate details of her personal life. Eventually those two rivers of my life began to converge together like a waterfall rushing over steep cliffs.

The dilemmas were very real and difficult for me. It was not simply a matter of trying to find a workable outline for a collaborative book project—no mean feat in itself. Rather, I was struggling very hard to live and work with the same degree of integrity and honesty that I saw Dagmar bringing to her life. Doing so meant that I could not ignore the deeper, darker currents of her life; but to write of them publicly, at least at that point in time, would have been politically dangerous, not to mention personally very painful, as I struggled to find my way as a member of Dagmar's larger family.

There is a profound spiritual truism I learned many years ago in struggling to come to grips with the historicity of the Bible: "All of these stories are True, and some of them really happened." It began to be clear to me that if I were to write the book that was lying like a pearl in the oyster of the streambed over which all of that water was rushing, I would have to do it myself, and I would have to write it as fiction. Someday I may still write that book, but at the time it was clear that that was not the book the Core Circle was working on, and that I was not the person to help them to do it. I avoided the plunge over the cliffs by getting out of the water and portaging into a different stream.

Now, we are all in very different places. But the dramatic and compelling story of Dagmar's life remains one that should be told, and one that should be heard by women in particular. I am more pleased than I can say that she has managed to put in writing these stories of her life.

The first time I met Dagmar, I was in awe of her feisty, critical spirit and, to be honest, intimidated by the strength of her intellect. I found myself fighting with her more often than agreeing with her, but the disagreements were always more interesting and more educational than simple affirmations would be.

She has never conformed to my expectations, whether of feminist work, political work, family work, or religious work. She is infuriating and loving—to such an intense and passionate degree that she draws people to her like a magnet. But that same magnetism draws critique and hatred as well. She has struggled with pain that is deep and wide but has kept her head mostly above water, using the rare submersions to help herself and others understand more of the ocean.

Postmodern theory suggests that, in many ways, we "make each other up." I have certainly been "made up" well in my encounters with Dagmar. What does it mean to be faithful and full of faith? To be a feminist and feminine? To be political and a politician? And to resist those terms? What does it mean to contest the way our culture has usually seen them and improvise new ways of understanding them? For me, that is the gist of who Dagmar is and is becoming. I guarantee that she will infuriate you, intrigue you, confuse you, and mystify you—but she will never bore you. And after having entered her life—even for just a short time in this book—you will come away changed.

Dagmar's mother, not quite having mastered English at the time, once proclaimed Dagmar's then husband, Dick, her "son-in-love." I am not sure if he would still merit that term in Oma's book, but I claim wholeheartedly, without reservation, Dagmar Celeste as my own "mother-in-love," and I hope that you will give yourself a chance to know her, too.

Preface

I began writing this book in early spring 1991 in response to the Kent State University Press's invitation to publish my life story. I was encouraged to put special emphasis on retracing my path from the banks of the Danube to the shores of Lake Erie; from a sophisticated young Viennese woman to an American foreign service spouse; from an ever-pregnant mother and persistent campaigner to the First Lady of Ohio, wife of the state's sixty-fourth governor.

I am a woman who was born, raised, and married in Austria; awakened in India; liberated, divorced, and now recovering in America. It is as a woman that I offer this story of my life, especially to other women. This is not a book about Ohio politics or the feminization of public policy; nor is it about recovery. This is simply a book about my attempt to fairly reconstruct some of the many stories I have lived so far.

I had three main reasons for spending more than a decade writing this: first and foremost, because the women in my Core Circle, the loyal friends who supported me when Dick was governor, encouraged me to write it; second, because no one else could do it for me; and third, because over time I came to believe that I could write it well enough. All I had to learn was to take myself lightly while taking my accomplishments seriously enough to dedicate real time and effort to pursuing my own truths. In fact, I was grateful for the opportunity to write this book, because by 1991 I had reached a point where reviewing my life seemed a worthwhile and timely challenge; it was a chance to rediscover myself and refine my memories.

I was never under the illusion that my story was all that different from other women's, and I am hopeful that my experiences will speak directly to the hearts of many women. In some ways my life has been charmed and privileged; in others it has been trying and even tortured. Like many, I have experienced the deep happiness of a longtime—if not lifelong—marriage. I have also experienced the exhilaration of giving birth to six healthy children, as well as the thrill of being present at the birth of five of our seven grandchildren. But like many women, I have also felt unhappiness and abandonment and thought I deserved no better. When I became so battle weary I could not go on, it was only to discover that even the worst emotional breakdowns can be transformed into spiritual breakthroughs. My willingness to embrace both pain and joy in these pages makes this more than a First Lady's fairy tale, and I hope the unhappy ending to my personal story will not detract from past accomplishments or the hard-won peace I have lately achieved.

I decided to tell my story in English because my ability to write in German, my mother tongue, or Italian, my father's language, has diminished considerably since I chose to become an American. I have worked hard to find the right words, relying on my fallible memory and with no research staff, historian, or ghostwriter to fall back on. If there are inconsistencies in this story, they are mine, and I take full responsibility for any lapses or omissions. This is, after all, my truth, no one else's. Whatever else this story is, however, I would not pretend that it represents the views of other family members, friends, or foes. This is simply my story told from my point of view, a point of view that, along with the story I set out to tell, kept changing even as I was writing.

The book is primarily a chronological narrative that spans half a century, beginning in 1941 with my childhood in Austria and ending with my leaving the Governor's Residence in 1991. The personal journal entries attempt to tell my story from a postdivorce perspective that spans four years, from August 1995 to August 1999.

The title "We Can Do Together" and the chapter titles come from our 1981 campaign song, "Have You Ever Seen the Sun Rise on Ohio?" which I commissioned Joe Ashley to write as a wedding anniversary gift for Dick in 1977. Throughout our marriage, the "we" in "We Can

Do Together" changed from the "we" of Dick and Dagmar to the "we" of us, our children, and their children and eventually to the "we" of the extended group of political and personal supporters. The "we" has also come to represent, for me, women's energy, so essential to my own survival—from my own mother, Theodora Braun, my grandmothers, Dora and Josephine, and my sister, Dorly, to my mother's friends and my own loyal women friends who have comforted and inspired me in so many ways.

During the first years of writing this book, Dick's commitment to our marriage and family was unquestioned. Ironically, when he asked me for a divorce just before Christmas 1994, I had just finished editing the chapter describing our pan-European courtship, which culminated in a fairy-tale wedding on August 24, 1962, in Dürnstein, Austria.

After Dick told me he wanted a divorce, I experienced the worst year of my life. Throughout 1995, I struggled to stay afloat, tossed among waves of self-pity, self-blame, fear, suicidal depression, and dark dreams of revenge. My desire to write shriveled and died. By Valentine's Day that year, I decided to hospitalize myself simply to protect those I love most from having to watch helplessly my descent into what seemed a bottomless well. On Easter Sunday 1995, I was well enough to go home for a visit; and after a few more weeks in the hospital, I finally began to get better for good, and late summer found me able to spend time at our house on Kelley's Island. As I became stronger, my desire to write returned.

The finality of my divorce from Dick at first seemed to have changed my story completely. I began to question every aspect of our time together. What had happened to that noble and caring young man I had fallen in love with more than three decades before? Where was that brilliant, glamorous woman he had loved so well and married? When did it all fall apart, and why?

What made everything even more confusing and painful were the reactions of people around me. I began to realize that by the 1990s in America, many people had come to believe that the promise of life-long solidarity, if not fidelity, need no longer stand in the way of fresh passion or the lure of a new love. The vow "Until death do us part" had been deconstructed to "Until we are no longer in love." "For better or worse" had become "Until I feel like leaving you."

Divorce felt worse than insanity. And while I recognized that recovering and forgiving are two sides of the same coin, I knew it would take much time to experience either. Writing helped me reclaim my own voice and take full responsibility for my points of view. At the end of the summer of 1995, instead of revising the main narrative to account for the unexpected end of our marriage, I began keeping a journal. Through that almost daily dialogue with myself, I found a fresh way to frame the story by adding my emerging new voice to the original narrative. That is why you will find me evoking both the present and the past in this book. The journal entries that precede each chapter include the date I reread and began to revise that particular section, along with some of my thoughts at the time.

My life has changed dramatically since I began this book. Today I am living alone in Cleveland. I have come to realize that my greatest challenge is to discover how Dick and I can best manifest our postdivorce connectedness and reconstruct our growing family ties; how I can become peaceful enough to acknowledge and affirm the "me" in any future "we" I might choose to consider; and how I can learn to live joyously in the here and now.

My fondest hope is to see—and help others see—that together we have much to celebrate and little to regret. Therefore, let me assure you that these written words were intended most of all to tell a love story—star-crossed and bittersweet, for sure, but a love story all the same. Audre Lorde once said, "Your silence will not protect you," and I'm aware that speaking from my heart won't either. I simply know that for the rest of my life I will stake my hopes on nothing less than the freedom to become the change I want to make and in humility and peace learn to live on in my own way.

Namaste/Shalom/Peace,
Dagmar

Acknowledgments

May your life become a daily pilgrimage and may you be satisfied
with nothing but the best. There is no rest till we reach the stars.
—Indira Devi

I thank Dora and Arthur Braun for giving me life and teaching me to
respect and honor all our Central European and Italian ancestors
whose sacrifices and sufferings in two world wars showed me that simply surviving will do. Thanks also to Maria and Elda Scrivanich, who
exposed me to a new world beyond Austria and taught me to respect
men and women willing to parent by choice rather than blood. Just
as those Italian sisters helped me appreciate Italy, so Frank and Peg
Celeste helped me to appreciate America. And, together with Steb
and Chet Bowles, they taught me the value of public life.

I owe a special debt of gratitude to all women of the First Lady's
Core Circle, especially Helen Fehervary, who first suggested we write
this book together, and Gloria Black, for deciphering and transcrib-
ing the initial interviews with the members of the Core Circle. Also,
thanks to Mary Hess for her valiant attempts to outline a possible version of this book. I am especially grateful to my first editor Gina Vild,
who recognized that I had stories to tell and encouraged me to write
a monthly First Lady column, and to Nikki Giovanni, for teaching
me that my story is at heart a love story. Thank you Letty Pogrebin
for suggesting the subtle subtitle.

Beginning with my first chief of staff, Gayle Channing, and ending
with Beverly L. Fay, my last, all members of the First Lady's unit were
key in helping me execute more ideas than I had a right to have. Now

that I have to staff myself, I am awed by how much we did together. Thank you Ruthmary Powers, Mike Tynen, Marvin Robinson, Roselyn Runnels, Patrice Lamblez, Beth Sliwowski, Sarah Straka.

Grateful blessings to the members of the theology group, especially Bobbie Celeste, who brought us together once a month at the Residence and kept us connected beyond the First Lady years. A tribute is due to Marlene Longenecker, for helping us create the Interagency Feminist Task Force, and to the many "femocrats" who served formally on it and continue to do informally the risky work of feminizing public policy within state government. You have my deepest appreciation.

Heartfelt thanks go to the Ohio Executive Residence staff, particularly Bobbie Wiard, the Residence security detail, the State Architect's office, and all the directors of DAS. I'm grateful to the many friends of the Residence, especially Les Wexner and Cookie and Victor Krupman, for helping Dick and me repair, restore, secure, and maintain that wonderful mansion we were privileged to call our home for eight years.

I respectfully acknowledge other former First Ladies, especially Hillary Clinton and the whole "Renaissance" tribe; Paula Blanchard, for setting the example with her well-written declaration of independence "'Til Politics Do Us Part"; Dottie Lamm, for her tongue-in-check "Second Banana"; and finally my predecessors, especially Helen Rhodes and Katie Gilligan, and successors, Janet Voinovich and Hope Taft.

With the help of my life coach Shirley Anderson and spiritual director Francis Teresa Wojnicki, I recommitted myself to the arduous task of writing the book on my own. My longtime friend Alicia Miller, a published author and professional book critic, became the anchor in the wild tossings of my imagination, while my sons Eric, Stephen, and Christopher and close friends Lee Ann Massucci and Mary Jo Ruggieri struggled valiantly to keep me from drowning in waves of depression.

The women on the Mary's Pence board were full of caring counsel. Father Sam Ciccolini hired me at the Internal Brotherhood Home as an addiction counselor. Linda Apple, Gloria Savage, Kay Eaton, the women in Sacred Space, Lynn MacCowan, Nancy J. Cullen, Rotraut Moslehner, Melody Bean, the members of my peer coaching group, Renee Nank, Mary Brown, Evelyn Hunt, and Carol Zung—the list is almost endless—all helped me stay the course. Carol Kumin's generous hospitality and help in editing are remembered with gratitude. So are David and Bonnie Millenthal, whose Passover gathering is the highlight of every spring for me. Also thanks to Debbie Phillips for her solid grief relief coaching and her insightful review of the final manuscript. Thanks to friends Anda Cook, Delia Burke, and Roberta Steinbacher. And special thanks to Joe Ashley for writing that great song—indeed, "we can do together"!

From the start, this book has been a partnership effort with Kent State University—especially Nancy Birk, the archivist in Special Collections, and Julia Morton and Joanna Hildebrand Craig, my editors at the Press—and with countless friends whose vision, support, and confidence sustained me through some rough-and-tumble times.

Last but not least, I want to thank Dick for his continued financial support, without which I could not have written this book, or spent as much time traveling with friends, visiting with my aging mother in Vienna, helping our kids and grandkids in Ohio and around the country, or serving the many worthy causes I choose to serve.

1

"Have you ever seen the
sun rise in Ohio?"

Keep your face to the sunshine
and you cannot see the shadow.
—*Helen Keller*

Himmelblau, Kelley's Island, Ohio
August 24, 1995

It was a morning like many others. Being an early bird I was up before sunrise. The rest of my family and friends were still soundly asleep at Himmelblau. We named our home on Kelley's Island Himmelblau because it means "sky blue" in German, which in turn translates to celeste *in Italian. Shortly after we bought the home, Ted, Dick's younger brother, told me how his German teacher at Lakewood High School started calling him Mr. Himmelblau. The story seemed funny and poignant then. That name connected the three most significant languages of my life: German, Italian and English—himmelblau, celeste, and blue heaven link the eternal expansiveness of clear blue skies with the deepest personal blue of my eyes and the magic of Pinocchio's blue fairy, the music of the blues and of the early Elvis's "Blue Moon" (my sister's favorite song) with late-summer Blue Moon roses.*

I moved about the kitchen as quietly as possible, fixing a cup of coffee, and began to bake bread. As I was kneading the dough, the calming, familiar rhythms freed my thoughts and memories. I found myself remembering the early mornings of my childhood, the sunrises my younger sister and I watched from the banks of the Danube and then, at age six, from the Trieste villa's balcony overlooking the Adriatic.

The memories of other sunrises filled my thoughts, as well.

I remember the first sunrise over the Danube following our wedding on August 24, 1962, at the Richard Loewenherz Inn in Dürnstein, Austria.

3

I remember the feeling of awe and elation as I experienced the sun rising while flying above the clouds high over the Atlantic on my way to America.

I remember morning breaking and a few rays of sun finding their way into that bright orange bedroom on Oak Street in New Haven, where we discovered ever new ways of lovemaking and where we conceived our first child.

I remember the sunrise illuminating that Washington Memorial Hospital room the morning I first held my newborn son Eric to my breast.

I remember that early morning flight into the sunrise on our way to Columbus, Ohio, on October 1, 1988, to welcome our first grandchild, Eleanor, into this world.

I remember many more sunrises—across the Cleveland skyline, over the pink stone buildings of New Delhi and Jerusalem, and over the calm lake waters of the Kashmir Valley, illuminating the rugged peaks of the Himalayan Mountains.

I remember the sunrise of four more births—Christopher, Gabriella, Noelle, and Natalie—and the rebirth of my crushed spirit in early 1979 at Mount Carmel Hospital in Columbus after the birth of our last child, Stephen, and the loss of our first race for governor.

And I remember one fine day when the sun rose on a cold January morning in 1983 to help us inaugurate Richard F. Celeste the sixty-fourth governor of the State of Ohio. That morning all our best hopes seemed to have been realized and our deepest doubts overcome. Together the whole family stood around the newly elected governor who was spouse, husband, father, brother, and son and heard him take an oath of office vowing to faithfully serve.

This morning at Himmelblau the sky was slowly changing from gray to crimson. I refilled my cup with steaming coffee, covered the bowl of fragrant bread dough waiting to rise, and rushed out of the house to greet the new sun. I watched and waited. But the tiny spark of bright light out beyond the waves didn't seem to change. I remained hopeful for a morning miracle, my soul silent but stirring, ready for a grand awakening. "If not the sun, then maybe a deer will appear to show the next step along the way,"

I thought. But in the dim pre-dawn light I saw nothing out of the ordinary—only tall grass and graceful cedars swaying in the morning breeze.

My mind was focused on watching my feet as I headed across the dew-soaked grass toward the barn behind the orchard. When I finally looked up, there they were, three deer. I was so close I could have touched one by simply lifting my hand. They, too, had stopped; their heads were raised high and they stood transfixed, gazing at the ordinary morning miracle awakening the world behind my back. I turned and saw the most brilliant sunrise of my life. My whole being was filled with its warm, pulsating light. The sun was just high enough in the sky to confront me face to face. For a few, still seconds, we were completed by each other's existence. I felt transformed.

Dora Braun gave birth to me on Sunday, November 23, 1941, in Krems a. d. Donau, a small Austrian town along the Danube, about an hour and a half by car west of Vienna, in the region called the Wachau, "the awakening wetland." I was born into a raging, warring world. Despite the horrors all around, my young (not yet nineteen) mother saw brightness, light. According to Mutti, Sunday children are lucky and bring good luck. She was relieved and happy and felt lucky to have a healthy baby. The year before she had given birth to a baby girl who died the next day. She, too, had been named Dagmar—a demonstration of either my mother's stubborn perseverance or an irrepressible liking for the name, or both. My father was disappointed. "Not another girl," he said, shortly before returning to battle. To him the world was one big battlefield, and he clearly wanted a son.

My earliest childhood memories are riddled with images of war. It was a difficult time. My mother and grandmother, with whom we lived, worked tirelessly to provide food and shelter. When my mother was just two years old, my grandfather, Vincent Prohaska, died, leaving my grandmother to support herself and her daughter. She worked variously as a seamstress, a secretary, and a housekeeper for an elderly ailing Jewish man. By the time I was in elementary school, she had become tourism director for the city of Krems. I remember fondly the long walks I took with my Oma and her huge dog Maedy along the banks of the Danube, listening to her extol the beauty of the Wachau region and tell stories of its past. She knew many people in Krems, and even more knew her. She was also an avid reader. But most of all she loved to sing.

My mother, too, had to work hard all her life. During the war, just before the Austrian currency was devalued, she managed to buy an orchard in Krems. All of us worked hard during the summer in our orchard, sold the fruit on market days, and saved the proceeds in order to buy food the rest of the year, and Mutti preserved cherries, apricots, red currants, and gooseberries. The orchard, with its small wood cabin, became our sustenance, our playground, our sanctuary. Many years later, the wise investment my mother made in that small piece of land became the foundation for family investments. Today, she lives in a beautiful villa in Vienna made possible because of her own wise planning and my father's frugality.

Often my sister, Utzi, and I used to play hide-and-seek in the natural caves near our orchard and the surrounding vineyards. One special cave where we spent many happy hours was just high enough for small children to enter. Inside, nature had shaped a table and two perfect benches. On hot afternoons, the caves were the only comfortable places to be, and during bombing raids they provided refuge.

One night in 1944, when I was about three years old, we barely made it to the orchard and inside the caves before a raid began. Up to then, I'd been too small to be frightened. Watching the faraway planes approach, listening to that faint engine noise come closer and closer and pass overhead—it was just another adventure. But that night the planes dropped their bombs so close to our sheltering cave that I could smell the smoke and dust and see the flames. That night I learned to fear for my life and hate war.

My godmother, Anna Steinbach Blei, suffocated in a building hit by one of those bombs. I can still hear my mother lament, "She was too young, too good, too beautiful to suffocate in flames and dust like some dog." I'm told Anni could not conceive a child and eventually adopted two sons, brothers. I was her only godchild and a girl and, therefore, very special to her. She used to spend hours pushing my baby carriage all over town. Yet on the day of my baptism, my grandmother had to take her place because Anni's husband refused to let her come to church. He was afraid to show his Catholic connections. In order to protect his Nazi credentials, he had even refused to marry Anni in the church. She had to agree to share her wedding day in a double ceremony at city hall with the Gauleiter, the Nazi leader of the occupied region. Anni was caught between her husband's politics and her faith. Her husband's refusal to marry her at the altar meant that she was denied Easter absolution year after year and denied a Catholic burial. It still enrages me to think that, between the cowardice of her husband and the hypocrisy of her church, Anni probably spent her last moments on earth in more terror of the world to come than fear of the one crumbling around her.

Anni died on Easter Sunday 1945. The American forces had dropped fliers on Good Friday announcing the upcoming offensive. The Allies' target was the train line along the Danube, one of the last functioning rail connections. For some reason, Anni decided to stay in her apartment rather than move to the shelter. I've often wondered why. Was she expecting someone? Was she waiting for someone to deliver food from the countryside? For whatever reason, she and her son Ulli were in their apartment when a bomb hit the nearby railroad station. The Americans had come early in the morning, bombing little else but their carefully chosen military targets, hitting and destroying the Donau Ufer-Bahn (the Danube Express Line) and a few apartment houses that were close to the railway tracks.

On reflection, I wonder if Anni was tired of running away, of hiding. Or maybe she just wanted to sleep a little longer, or finish her breakfast. Mutti tells me that Anni was full of life, love, and sparkle; she was fun, young, and beautiful and certainly did not want to die. But she was not a happy woman. She had an unhappy marriage and a married lover. Her husband, a very stern and judgmental man, did not attend her funeral or attempt to make arrangements for a proper grave. Her lover saw to Anni and Ulli's burial in the town where they died. After the war, Anni's mother moved their bodies to her hometown graveyard.

• • •

After my father's last leave home, in the spring of 1942, my mother found herself pregnant. In December 1942 she gave birth to my sister, Utzi. Officially baptized Theodora, after my mother and grandmother, my sister was named Utzi by me. It seems I could not pronounce such a long complicated name and kept trying to call her Putzi, which means "baby" in German; but it came out Utzi.

At war's end, my father was listed as missing. My mother continued the struggle of keeping two little girls alive until Vati (Daddy) finally returned. I discovered many years later that he managed to desert from the German army and disappear into Italy. As much as Vati and I disagreed on almost everything in later years, there was one thing we did agree on: all wars are useless at best; we tend to become what we fight, and every victory only paves the way for future wars.

When the bombs finally stopped falling on lower Austria, those of us who managed to survive the heat of the battle were now delivered into the icy contempt of the Russian occupational forces. Now it was the former Nazis who were on the run. During that time, Mutti said, women were loyal friends and desperately tried to hide each other's sons—during the war from the concentration camps and after D-Day from deportation to Siberia. When I asked Mutti why she had risked her life to hide an SS man, Anni's brother, she told me she did it for Anni's mother. "Losing her only daughter was enough. I just wanted to help her keep her only son alive. After all, what are women friends for if we don't try to save each other's children?"

Women caught in the middle of wars struggle against almost overwhelming odds to survive. At the end of the war, my mother was twenty-two years old; I was three and a half, and Utzi was two and a half. Mutti was on her own, responsible for all of us. She was very beautiful and therefore always at risk. I don't know how many times she was raped, but I do know that for her the war was not over when the shooting stopped. For women, the streets were as dangerous during the occupation as they had been during the air raids. American soldiers were more popular because at least they could afford to reward the women and girls they chose to ravish. In those days, nylon stockings, chocolate, chewing gum, peanut butter, Spam—any food, for that matter—and most important of all, cigarettes, were in such high demand that women could seldom resist and often could not afford to say no. Furthermore, if they did, they only ended up being forced to provide the service without being compensated. Conquest of geographic territory often seems to extend to rape of women and abuse of children, as well as the theft of material things. The biblical curse cited in the charge given to Adam was to subdue the earth. It is interesting that Eve's curse to bear children in pain did not grant her ownership of those children or even ownership of her own body. For men, the curse sanctioned exploitation and oppression: men could sell and buy land, women, and children and keep the profit.

But men, too, are brutalized by war and suffer the same damage as those victims who are sexually and mentally tortured. Dehumanization at all levels is a constant companion of military conquests. So I am puzzled by women who applaud their warrior fathers, husbands, lovers, brothers, and sons. I dream that one day women all over this earth will become strong enough to protect themselves and their children and become wise enough to see the enemy's children as part of one united, extended family. I hope that one day we will find the courage to stop our men from fighting bloody wars and promoting violent revolutions. We givers of life must at least refrain from cheering them on into death.

One of my saddest childhood memories is Christmas 1946, when the Russian officers living in our home (the living room of our one-bedroom apartment was commandeered by the occupation force for use by its officers) stole all our Christmas presents to send to their own children in Russia. Today, I have some empathy for those young, lonely, uneducated, starving Russian troops; but at the time they seemed like monsters, and the mere sight of a Russian uniform could make me sick. It's amazing how strong those early impressions were. Many years later, while we were living and working in India, Russian astronaut Yuri Gagarin made an official visit to New Delhi. In those Cold War days, no high-ranking American embassy official was permitted to participate at the welcoming ceremonies. But the wife of the ambassador's assistant was insignificant enough to be sent to represent the American embassy. As luck would have it, my seat was right behind the astronaut's; unfortunately, he arrived in full military regalia. Upon seeing the Russian uniform, I became violently ill and had to excuse myself. I sincerely hope no one saw it as an official snub by the United States.

. . .

Despite the violence, the fear, and the near-starvation, my childhood was filled with good times, and I never thought of myself as poor. My mother managed to provide us not only with food and security but also with toys and books, all handmade. Mutti made us our books. She wrote the stories, and her best friend, Lisel, a fine artist, illustrated them with primroses, bluebells, fairies, and always a ladybug for good luck. I remember loving a teddy bear that was made from my grandmother's old fur coat. It seemed to me, at the time, that we lacked very little.

Yet, bath time proved us poor! Every Friday night, the whole family bathed in a portable tub in the middle of the kitchen, and only once a week could we afford to heat enough water to fill the tub. It took quite a few buckets of water to fill up our tub. And since we had only one bucket and two large pots, and with wood and coal hard to come by, heating enough water for the family baths became a weekly challenge. We always battled over who would get to take the first bath. (I knew for a fact that if my little sister got to go first, she would pee as soon as she sat down in the warm water.)

As much as I loved my little sister, we did our fair share of fighting and troublemaking. Whenever my mother would go out for the evening with one of her women friends, to a movie or to play cards or to just escape from the housework, we were left by ourselves. We relished these evenings as much as she did. This was our chance to dance on the windowsills while horrified passersby tried frantically to convince us to get down or an opportunity to fill paper bags with water and drop them on the heads of unsuspecting victims. We were beyond mischievous and were nicknamed Max and Moritz after the two naughty boys in a popular German adventure story.

Some of my fondest childhood memories are of going for walks with my mother and sister and making up fairy tales. My mother would begin by asking us to give her a cast of characters, which usually included some dwarfs, a giant, a dragon, a fairy, a witch, and talking trees or magical animals. And little girls were *always* the heroes, and they *always* won in the end. And there were *always* happy endings. In retrospect, I realize how well these tales conditioned me to believe in dreams and magic and to hope against all odds for happy endings always.

2

"Have you ever seen
Ohio in the fall?"

Ich lebe mein Leben in wachsenden Ringen
die sich ueber die Dinge ziehen.
ich werde den letzten vielleicht nicht vollbringen,
aber versuchen will ich ihn.

I live my life in growing circles
which cover everything.
I may not complete the final one,
but try I will.
—*Rainer Maria Rilke*

Columbus, Ohio
October 22, 1995

On the way to Ann Arbor to celebrate our daughter Gabriella's twenty-ninth birthday, I was listening to a tape of the book Awakenings. *The author, Oliver Sacks, describes the ravaging effects of sleeping sickness and Parkinson's disease and the almost miraculous but temporary effects of L-dopa, a drug discovered in the late 1960s. I thought of Chester Bowles, who had been Kennedy's ambassador to India and had been part of the L-dopa experiment. He had given us the rare opportunity to work with him for four years in India. He was my first male mentor. In fact, he was more like my champion, and, together with his wife, Steb, he helped both Dick and me to grow and thrive, personally and politically. Chet eventually succumbed to Parkinson's disease, and Steb embarked on a recovery road from alcoholism in her seventies. They both inspired me by living the fall and winter years of their lives with humor and ever-deepening hope and acceptance.*

Thinking of Chet and Steb brings back memories of better times, when our children were still small, our dreams still alive, our hardships still manageable, and when we were filled with a passion for living. Now, in the autumn of my life, the shadows have deepened, and despite the bright fall foliage all around me my spirit seems to have broken both wings. The decay, dysfunction, and destruction brought about by our divorce have crept into every crevice of my being and are threatening even my capacity to enjoy nature's fall and her simple gift of beauty.

Before I came to Ohio thirty-three years ago, spring was my favorite season. And then Dick Celeste, this tall and charismatic Ohioan whom

15

I had fallen in love with and married, introduced me to the wonders of Ohio's autumn. Little did I realize then the spiritual significance of such a transformation. The change of allegiance from spring to fall changed my whole way of life. I moved from being a person who valued exuberance to a woman who slowly began to learn to accept her limits. Day by day the enthusiasms of spring transformed into the growing courage of fall. The freedom of youth gave way to the responsibilities of adulthood. On that journey I developed a deeper sense of belonging and created for myself, my spouse, and my children more home ground to stand on, more fertile soil for nourishment.

One of my favorite places in Ohio is Malabar Farm, writer Louis Bromfield's home in Pleasant Valley. When war broke out in Europe, Bromfield returned to Ohio, his place of birth. He purchased the farm and began what is now known as contour farming. The system of tilling the land requires more effort initially but protects and enhances the soil eventually. The traditional farmers around him dismissed his new, unproven experiments. A decade later, Malabar Farm's fields had ten inches more topsoil than the fields of those who farmed strictly according to tradition. Over the years, I had come to view my marriage the way Bromfield viewed his land, using a form of contour cultivation—shoring the field up all around but leaving it free to breathe and grow and protecting it from erosion without suffocating it with unrealistic expectations. Learning to accept my powerlessness over out-of-control passions was yet another step along this seasonal journey that lasted thirty-three years. So far, my harvest has been six children and four grandchildren and the memories of a constructive and creative partnership and friendship.

Some of my fondest Ohio fall memories are woven into almost two decades of Willaloo gatherings. The name Willaloo means "great commotion" in one of the many Native American languages and was an apt name for those great, moving, noisy times. Patterned after the Bowles's annual Memorial Day weekends, our group of family and political friends, dubbed "Celestials" by the Ohio media, came together the weekend after Labor Day in one of Ohio's extraordinary state parks to plot political strategies and plan new campaigns. We worked hard for a day and then just played and had fun together. By the time Dick left the governor's office, we had celebrated our twentieth Willaloo anniversary.

When Dick decided to leave home, I was at first hopeful that not all personal and political rituals of the past, such as Willaloo, would be lost. But I was wrong. The death of his mother had made him fearful of his own autumn and of the winter to come. He found consolation in the arms of a woman the age of his daughters. Out went the wife of thirty-three years, mother of his six children and grandmother of his grandchildren. Thirty-three years of personal, and more than twenty years of political, common causes could not withstand the cold wind of unresolved grieving and unchecked fear of death. Conscience, community, and constituency concerns vanished from his consciousness, and our love became a dim memory, if that.

Ironically, my parents' wedding anniversary occurs on the same fall day Dick has chosen to remarry. On that day, October 28, 1995, the happy couple will have to compete with "Indian fever" in Cleveland. I wonder how many of his buddies will trade the World Series for this latest Celeste kickoff?

But by the time I celebrate my birthday, which this year coincides with Thanksgiving, I will try to gratefully remember the many gifts still left to me—my mother, my teachers, my mentors, my friends, my children, my grandchildren. I choose to believe that the old woman who is emerging this fall season continues to have in her the strength of the girl who survived foreign occupation and war, the stamina of the wife who survived betrayals and desertion, and the passion of the mother who conceived, birthed, and raised six children. I need to take comfort more often in how much I have overcome thus far. I need to remind myself that despite living with parents wounded by war and a spouse blindsided by lust, we managed to nurture six sane, courageous, and sometimes even serene men and women.

Those first years of postwar occupation were incredibly difficult. Food was scarce, and health care was virtually nonexistent. In 1947, the Red Cross developed a program enabling children who lived in countries that had lost the war to travel and stay with families in countries that had won. Since Italy had switched sides at the very end of the war, and the Marshall Plan supplies were sent to Allies first, the Red Cross decided to send to Italy those Austrian children who were sick or starving. To be eligible for the program, a child had to be the oldest in the family and had to be sufficiently malnourished. I qualified on both counts. Since my father was born in Trieste, Italy, and had relatives and friends living there, it seemed natural that my parents allowed me to participate in this program.

The separation was very painful, and the trip was horrible. In the middle of winter, we lonely, homesick children traveled south in a very small, old, unheated bus. We cried our way across the Alps. Leaving home felt like exile; all I could think about was my mother and how sad she looked when we had to say good-bye.

The host families who had volunteered to take children were waiting at the bus station in Trieste. I refused to leave the bus and insisted that I wanted to return home. I was very frightened when a large woman in a fur coat approached to coax me off the bus. All I could think was, "My God, she looks like a bear. I don't want to stay with someone who looks like a bear." Her fur coat reminded me of those worn by the Russian soldiers, and that connection was hardly reassuring. Somehow the woman in the fur coat—Zia Maria, as I came to call her later on—managed to take me from the bus to her car, and Nicco, her driver, sped away toward my new home—a small, beautiful villa in Servola overlooking the Adriatic.

They first took me to her downtown apartment, where she had accumulated in the kitchen an assortment of toys the likes of which I had never seen. There was a dollhouse, a couple of dolls, some doll furniture including a carriage, and Pinocchio. Despite this wealth of toys, my eyes were drawn to a large bowl filled with oranges on the kitchen table. I thought they were apples—strange apples, to be sure—but until that moment I had never seen an orange. I rushed and grabbed a piece of fruit and bit into it. It tasted nothing like an apple. Bright red juice squirted into my face, and my hands were red and sticky. "It's just a blood orange," Zia Maria reassured me when she saw my shock. But the word "blood" only made matters worse. "What horrible place is this," I screamed, "where apples are full of blood?!" It took a long time for her to calm me down.

To distract me, she and Nicco finally decided to take me for a drive to see the harbor. It was evening, and the ocean liners anchored in the harbor were lit up like Christmas trees. But nothing could cheer me so far away from home. Still, the thought of Christmas did help me to go to sleep that first night. I don't remember how long I continued to cry myself to sleep, but after three months I began to understand and even speak some Italian, and my thoughts of home, Mutti, Utzi, and Oma slowly became less painful.

Over time, I settled in and came to love this new home. Vineyards surrounded the house, and the small garden was filled with geraniums and potted oleander trees. Every summer Maria's sister Elda would plant rows and rows of geraniums and carefully tend the flowering trees. At the back of the house was a large peach tree, and I remember spending many happy hours eating as many ripe, juicy peaches as I liked. And the entrance to the garden was graced by an almond tree. Only once did I see it in bloom; but every summer I came to enjoy its fruit. In addition to being a loving, gifted gardener, Elda also was a fine cook. Her artichokes, spaghetti sauce, fried sardines, grilled mackerels, and special way of fixing tripe with polenta remain to this day some of my favorite foods.

Maria Scrivanich was a medical doctor and her sister, Elda, was a retired schoolteacher. Zia Maria was short and heavy, but somehow her size was reassuring rather than overwhelming. She dressed conservatively but quite expensively, though there was nothing frivolous about her appearance. Her suits were simple, her jewelry unobtrusive, and her black doctor's bag sturdy and of quality leather. Her gray hair was well cut and gently permed, and her nails were always manicured—buffed, not polished. She wore no makeup. I had never met a woman who had more class, or at least what I took for class at that young age. I discovered later that she was quite famous for prescribing arthritis remedies based on a formula her physician father had left her on his deathbed. People came from all over Italy to take her series of shots, which seemed to bring them relief from pain.

Upon my arrival, Zia Maria went to work on my health, and Zia Elda focused her energy on my nutrition and education. Three meals a day, milk, and fresh fruits and vegetables, as well as biweekly calcium shots, helped me get back on my feet. After three months of food and rest, Elda started me on reading and piano lessons. Zia Maria was fun-loving and friendly; Zia Elda was pragmatic and serious and rather intimidating. I slept in Maria's room—in her big double bed—and she cared for me like a mother. I came to love her very much. To this day I still pray the little evening prayer she taught me:

Vieni, vieni
Gesu bambino
a posare il tuo capino
sul guanciale del mio letto
vieni, vieni
che t'aspetto
vieni, vieni
non tardare
senza te non posso stare

Come, come
Jesus child
and rest your little head
on my pillow.
Come, come

I am waiting, don't delay.
Come, come,
don't be late
because I cannot live without you.

The greatest challenge was learning a new language. Maria spoke just a bit of German, and Elda spoke none. Even as a little girl I understood that, in order to learn Italian well, I had to risk losing my own mother tongue. And sure enough, by the time I was healthy enough to return home to Austria a year later, my Italian was fluent but my German had suffered. Year after year, I spent my summer vacations in Trieste and in the fall returned to Austria for the school year. I felt displaced much of the time, missing my mother and sister while in Italy and Zia Maria when in Austria.

With Zia Maria I not only learned Italian but also learned to love Italy, its culture, its people, and especially its food. She, more than anyone else, introduced me to the great big world outside my family. Together we traveled. She took me to Venice, Pisa, Padua, the mountains, the ocean, and many other places within driving distance. On the way to the mountains, we would pass the cemeteries for fallen soldiers at Redipuglia, and we always stopped at their home village of Sagrado and visited the small country cemetery to clean up the tomb of Maria's father and mother and her little brother. Years later, after leaving the Governor's Residence in 1991, I made my way there again, to carry out those simple rituals in honor of the two sisters who had become such an important part of my life so long ago. There at Sagrado, on the banks of the Tagliamento, surrounded by tall cypress trees, the whole Scrivanich family now rests in peace.

One of my brightest memories of Zia Maria was our visit to Padua. I was eight or nine years old. When Zia Maria attended the university, she was the only woman in her graduating class and one of only half a dozen female medical doctors in all of Trieste. Maria took me to the medical school, showed me her favorite lecture halls, and introduced me to some very old professors. At this point, she was in her late forties and quite famous in her own right, and I fondly remember how those academic men treated her with great respect. I also remember very clearly how proud I was to be with her—so proud that I decided then and there that I wanted to grow up to be just like her. Somehow, in my teens, I forgot that resolve and became sidetracked by personal rebellions and boys.

After my visit with Maria to the university, we went to Saint Anthony's tomb. (Upon reflection, I realize that Saint Anthony must have been her favorite saint, for every Sunday we attended Mass at St. Antonio Nuovo in the heart of Trieste, even though there were other churches much closer to the villa.) She walked me around the saint's tomb and told me the story of how Anthony protects the poor. She then placed my hand on the tombstone and said, "He will protect you, too, because he loves children very much."

Much later in my life, while living in Cleveland, I met the Zannoni family and discovered that they had donated an altar dedicated to Saint Anthony at Saint Rocco's, an Italian neighborhood parish on Cleveland's West Side. Every election day, Dick and I would begin the day with some quiet meditation and lighting of candles in front of that altar. It seemed strange to me at first that Dick was so drawn to that particular saint, since Methodists aren't known for lighting candles. Years later, when I suffered postpartum depression and Dick was deeply concerned, he went to Saint Rocco's to collect his thoughts and garner strength to help us through that trying time.

Zia Maria lived long enough to meet my husband and my first baby, Eric. She seemed happy for me, if a bit disappointed that I had married after all and wasted my talents. At the end of her life, she was sick and lonely. And despite all the effort and love she had put into raising me and helping others, she died alone, with none of us even at her funeral. I found out about her death almost six months after it happened, when Adriana, the daughter of one of her ex-maids, took the time to find me and write. I never had the opportunity to thank Maria for her love and for the example she had set.

She taught me much about prayer and mystery. On our many

weekend trips, she would pull out her rosary and begin mystery by mystery, decade by decade, to recite what seemed to me then an unending stream of Ave Marias. Nicco and I were expected to become "the people chorus," responding to her leads. This way, bead by bead, Maria Scrivanich taught me the value of paying attention to life's mysteries and the power inherent in Mary, the mother of God, and how she connects to the healing power in nature and in all women.

Today I wonder how I could have so long forgotten the fervor that I had felt at Padua to live a life of my own. Today I also understand that my insatiable thirst for knowledge and truth and my love for and appreciation of my own gender come from that early childhood experience of growing up protected in the shadow of these great and good women.

· · ·

The Roman Catholic Church declared 1950 a holy year. This was also the year I received First Communion and, later, was confirmed in Trieste. Professor Redel was my religion teacher in elementary school. For almost a full year she diligently prepared us for our First Communion. While she also had to prepare us for our First Confession, her emphasis was always more on grace and original blessing than on sin and punishment. She made First Communion such a special privilege that, when the day arrived, I was filled with the excitement and anticipation of ten Christmas Eves. I especially remember her telling us the story of Fabiola, who, as a very young girl, so desired Communion that the host floated to her from the altar to the amazement of a stunned priest who was left empty-handed. Just that day he had forbidden her to receive Communion because she was too young.

And so finally my great day dawned. I and my friends stood before the ornate baroque altar of the Kremser Pfarrkirche (parish church) in beautiful white dresses and with fresh flowers in our hair. I barely heard Reverend Goetschner's sermon explaining the mysteries of transubstantiation, but I vividly remember the feeling of palpable happiness. I also remember one distinct, mystical moment in the ceremony. The sun must have finally broken through the cloudy day. A single ray penetrated the large stained-glass window, exploded into multiple facets, and landed, like a shower of rainbows, on the steps leading up to the altar. I took this splendid display as a special message from God. As I stepped through this curtain of many-colored lights on my way up the steps to receive my first taste of "soul food," I promised myself to always protect this secret place inside me where I would remain an innocent and untouched virgin forever, and only the Divine could enter and play. That day a deep, silent, sacred space opened in me, and I knew that a beloved Divine had chosen my humble heart as home. That deep reverence, while fleeting at times, has stayed with me.

Then I was back among my many girlfriends, eager to get to the next stage of the festivities, especially the grand breakfast awaiting us in the parish hall. Those were the days when we had to fast from sundown until we received Communion, so I suppose some will assume that all those glorious visions of rainbow colors and special consummation were created by sleeplessness and fasting. I look back at that ritual and realize how significant such celebrations are, especially for girls. First Communion and, later, confirmation were coming-of-age rituals that helped me experience a sense of belonging—to creation, the Creator, and myself. In receiving these sacraments, I was shown that only those able to be open to the love of the spirit of life can learn to love themselves, and only those willing to love themselves gently can love others gracefully.

I spent my summer vacation of 1950 in Italy, as usual, and Zia Maria found for me Anita Tomaselli, a most wonderful confirmation sponsor. Together they arranged for my confirmation at San Antonio Nuovo after taking me to Padre Pieter for a special confession. With my confirmation, my sense of autonomy deepened. To become a full member of the Catholic community, I had to rename myself and accept full responsibility for my own spiritual welfare and that of the whole Church. I chose my sponsor's first name, Anita, for my own confirmation name. Today I can see the subtle name thread connecting me from baptism to confirmation, from Anna to Anita. When I look at photographs of that little girl all dressed in white, so much like a bride, I hardly recognize her. But I'll never forget her feelings that marvelous day: she was special and strong, and she knew it; she was chosen to be a warrior of the spirit, and she accepted the commission enthusiastically.

I felt a similar sense of anointment in 1962, at our wedding, and again twenty years later at the inauguration of my best friend, lover, and spouse as the governor of the State of Ohio. At the inaugural service at Saint Joseph's Cathedral in Columbus, I chose to read the Beatitudes. Once more I felt a special call to deepen my sense of mission and to dedicate the next four (or more) years, and possibly the rest of my life, to serve others, especially women and children, those rejected, dejected, addicted, and those locked up in state prison cells or in prisons of their own making.

In the rituals of my life, I have always been surrounded by the tender care of women. My mother sewed the special dress for First Communion and, later, my bridal gown. My grandmother found ways to make events unique with music. My theology teachers, special women all, impressed on me the preciousness of my innocence as well as a compassion for my own and other people's failings and weaknesses. And my confirmation was mediated through the grace-filled partnership of two women, Maria and Anita. Neither of them had a child of their own, yet they knew how to be spiritual anchors to the daughter they had wished to birth.

Perhaps it was because of their own childless states that they had developed a generosity deep enough to reach out to all children, especially me, with such selfless loving. Every year, when I came for vacation, Maria and Anita would take me shopping. They would always ask, "What is it you *really* want this year?" Although my parents provided well for me, they seldom—if ever!—asked me about my true heart's desire. When it came to clothes, my father insisted on the best quality; it had to be real cotton or wool or leather and deemed sturdy and durable. (My sister and I had very few things, but those few items were always the best.) So, of course, my pleas for a red plastic purse were met with disapproval; only cheap women wore red plastic. Once I returned to Trieste, however, I got my wish: a red purse (leather, I admit, but very bright red) and my first lipstick to match. Anita and Maria also took me to restaurants, where they let me order exactly what I wanted—usually fried calamari. Never once did they belittle or criticize my choices. They seemed to take great pleasure in simply fulfilling my most extravagant childhood wishes.

It was from that experience that I learned the importance of giving my own children real choices. When it came to playthings and clothing, I tried to provide real choices even when they were still very small. Also, the example Maria and Anita provided in working together for my confirmation was what helped me decide to prepare each one of my children for First Communion with the help of religious women friends. But when or even whether to be confirmed I left open for them to decide.

I do believe women have a special talent for creating rituals that celebrate the spiritual significance of life's passages. We celebrate the high feasts as well as the more common, everyday events. We make noteworthy our passage into womanhood and the liberation of menopause and the autonomy of old age. In ancient goddess spirituality, the trinity is divided into virgin, mother, and crone: the virginity is seen as autonomous, self-sufficient; the mother as fertile and capable of creating and nurturing; and the crone as wise. Only in celebrating these life-stages can we fully connect with our creative selves, with other women, and with the power of female energy.

· · ·

Trieste has been significant, sacred ground throughout my life. In addition to my own connection, my father's family has deep roots in that city. My grandmother, Josephine Maria Blasic, was born on March 19, 1877, in Trieste and lived in Via Madonnina. She married Stefan Braun, who was born November 20, 1876, in Zagreb and was postmaster general for the Austro-Hungarian monarchy and stationed at Miramare, a romantic castle overlooking the Adriatic. They wed on

April 30, 1901, in the diocese of Tergestina. Nine years later, October 2, 1910, my father, Arthur Braun, was born in Trieste. He was the youngest of three children; Melitta and Egon were his older siblings. Egon became an outstanding philosophy professor at the University of Vienna and one of the most renowned Aristotle scholars of Europe. My father, while a good student and later a noted lawyer, always felt inferior to his older brother.

My father was as cynical as Egon was idealistic. During Hitler's rise to power, Egon, who was a true believer in the myth of the thousand-year Reich, became an officer, while my father, who believed in neither God nor the Führer, remained a lowly soldier. Saved from front-line duty by his linguistic abilities—he spoke fluent German, Italian, Slovenian, and French—he served as a translator for the Germans in Malo, a small village close to Verona, Italy.

Years later, when he and my mother visited Malo, the villagers gave him a hero's welcome. They credited him with saving their lives. At the end of the war the Germans were anxious to capture the many partisans hiding in the woods around the village. The partisans communicated by short-wave radio—in Italian, of course—and my father was expected to translate those communications. At first he provided accurate translations; he then discovered that those who were captured were hung in the village's main square, right in front of his window. Thereafter he mistranslated the messages, often diverting the Nazis away from where he knew the partisans to be. Vati told us that he only did it because he didn't want to wake up every morning to such unpleasantness. To his family he was a broken, bitter man who rarely shared his memories, though he was haunted by them until his final days; but to the villagers of Malo, he was a savior. Perhaps they understood him better than we did.

When Vati received orders to join Rommel's Afrika Corps, he decided to desert. He left the transport train in Verona and stayed in Italy, hiding at the home of a friend. When he finally returned home from the war, he found a position with the Chamber of Commerce of Lower Austria, and he eventually rose to become its chief legal counsel. His greatest professional disappointment was his inability to become president of the chamber, primarily because he was betrayed by a man he had helped up that very same career ladder. His greatest personal sadness was the breakup of a prewar love affair with a beautiful, talented opera singer who chose an older, richer suitor who could better further her career. While Vati's love for her must have diminished over the years, his love for music, especially romantic operettas, never died. At the end of his life, the radio was his constant companion, and the voices of various sopranos seemed his only pleasure.

I'm sure my father loved my mother and respected her common sense and her willingness to work hard, as well as her incredible commitment to us children. But she was not the great love of his life. Furthermore, he was not an easy man to be married to. Over the years, he had numerous affairs. The time my mother attempted to commit suicide—according to her, just to get his attention—he barely reacted. That day my sister and I returned from school to find our apartment's front door lock broken. We were taken in by our neighbor, my mother's friend Lia Stadler, and told us that Mutti had been rushed to the hospital. After coming home from work that night, my father's only comment was, "Why did they have to break down the door?"

3

"The farmlands and the towns,
the busy city sounds,
Seems to me Ohio has it all"

I did not know that God is in all things.
—*Teresa of Avila*

Mohican State Park, Ohio
Summer 1995

Louis Bromfield used to say about Ohio that it is the farthest east of the west and the farthest west of the east, the farthest south of the north and the farthest north of the south. Buckminster Fuller places Ohio and the Great Lakes region in the central triangle of his dymaxion air-ocean world map, linking all the other triangles that make up his fresh way of seeing geographic reality.[1]

In 1998, Dick asked David Millenthal, his media consultant, and other advisers to create a new state slogan. The brainstorming went on for hours. Since Buckminster Fuller's map was prominently displayed on one of the walls of the governor's office, I began to search first for Ohio and then for Austria, which has long viewed itself "at the heart of Europe." "Ohio—at the heart of America" sounded too awkward. "The heart of America." Which America—North or South? "At the heart of the Americas." On and on I scribbled variations of the theme on my notepad. The campaign song began to play in my head: "Seems to me, Ohio has it all." Excited discussion led to consensus; everyone agreed that "Ohio, the heart of it all" should be the state's new motto.

. . .

Recently I joined in celebrating the tenth anniversary of Children First, the day care center for state employees located in the Riffe Center in Columbus.

1. The dymaxion map shows our planet without any visible distortion of relative shapes and sizes of the land and sea areas and without any breaks in the continental contours.

That center was the result of the determined, persistent efforts of Dick and me and such key players as Gayle Channing from my staff and Bill Sykes from the governor's cabinet. The gathering evoked many bittersweet memories. In the display of photographs there was a picture of Dick playing with the center's children; I was off to the side, almost outside of the picture, holding our first grandchild, Eleanor, who was no more than six months old.

Christopher, her dad, was my escort for the anniversary celebration and the family representative. Marvin Robinson, my former communications director and now partner at Himmelblau House, also joined me in representing the many First Lady staff members who were part of the team that built Children First. But I missed Gayle, Marlene Longenecker, and Beverly Luciow-Fay, the three key people who, more than anyone else, helped me transform mere wishes into real programs, mere thoughts into polished speeches, and simple caring into lasting public policies. These Ohio women were at the heart of it all. And I also felt a deep longing to share the joy of this small victory with my best friend and former spouse. I thought of the countless other beautiful and true Celestial companions who, together with us, came to believe that "with God all things are possible."

One of the first people I met at the celebration was ten-year-old Linda Oxenrider. Her mother was searching through the many photo albums that showed the rich life of the center over the last decade and discovered a picture of Linda from years ago. I asked Linda what she remembered of her four-year stay at Children First. She smiled shyly and said, "The elevator . . . and snack time."

O n May 15, 1955, the Allied Forces signed a final peace treaty that gave Austria a new start. After Stalin's death, the Soviets were ready to loosen the reins a bit. Austria, because of its ability to pull all political factions together through a coalition government comprised of socialists and conservatives, and because of its willingness to become a neutral nation, was therefore able to rid itself of all occupying forces.

I remember standing in the garden at the Belvedere Palace in Vienna, a thirteen-year-old girl watching our Austrian leaders join the leaders of the four Allied Forces on the balcony. When they lifted up the freshly signed document assuring Austria's independence and freedom, the crowd was still and silent. But only for a moment. Then the very ground under my feet shook from the sudden roar of the crowd. The air was filled with the cheers and jubilation of thousands of schoolchildren and adults. I understood then that such miracles of liberation come about only when leaders are willing to cooperate and with the disciplined, patient participation of a people ready for major change. I think the experiences and sensations of that day, of the Staatsvertrag, laid the foundation for my faith in the democratic process and my commitment to peaceful politics.

The last Allied soldier left Austria on October 26, 1955. That same day, the National Assembly declared Austria's permanent neutrality. Austria also accepted the stipulation that it never unite economically or politically with Germany and promised to recognize the rights of Slovenian and Croatian minorities within her borders. By December 15, 1955, Austria had become a member of the United Nations.

We had moved to Vienna in 1951, just in time for the Staatsvertrag. Utzi and I were sent to high school at the Humanistic Gymnasium in the Gymnasiumsstrasse in Doebling. Never the academic type, Utzi quit school a year later and chose to apprentice as a dental technician; she preferred the more concrete, hands-on work of a trade. Her decision was a courageous one because she had little support from anyone in our family. When she left the Gymnasium, my father became that much more determined that I would follow in his footsteps and become a lawyer.

It was at about this same time that my parents' marriage began to crumble. They fought all the time, and divorce appeared inevitable, and even desirable. After my mother's failed suicide attempt, she decided to get a job, so Utzi and I were packed up and sent off to an all-girls boarding school in Vienna. This came as a relief to us, because at least we were removed from the battle on the home front.

While there, I developed a serious crush on one of my female instructors, Eva W. She returned my feelings in an innocent, caring way and helped to boost my self-confidence. She was the youngest teacher at our boarding school and, by contrast, the other instructors seemed dull and rigid. Before I met Eva, I had had crushes on my first-grade teacher and also on one of my mother's friends. I believe it's only natural for girls, especially when confined to mostly female settings, to experience infatuation of that sort. But my feelings for Eva were stronger; for me her mere entrance into a room brought with it light and warmth. If she brushed up against me or lightly touched my shoulder, chills ran up and down my spine.

Meanwhile, life at home had become more and more difficult, with my parents now locked in combat; I dreaded even the weekend visits. Mutti was very distracted, and while she did her best to reassure us of her love, I felt insecure and confused. Compared to Krems, Vienna was a big city, and everything was still strange and new to me.

Yet in Eva's presence I felt safe and whole. Our relationship was innocent, never sexual. The closest we came to physical intimacy was a simple good-night kiss; before turning out the lights, she would come over to my bed, tuck me in, and gently kiss me on the forehead. Once I remember her sitting down long enough to share a smile and to say the most loving thing I had ever heard up until then: "One day," she whispered, "I hope to have a daughter as wonderful as you." Because of Eva's gentle, unconditional love, my shattered self began to mend and my fragile self-confidence to strengthen and grow.

One evening after dinner, Eva invited me to her room to read some poetry. The phone rang. It was Dr. Popper, her supervisor, and she wanted to know whether I was with her. Unfortunately, Eva denied my presence. When she hung up the phone, she turned out the light and, to my complete astonishment, asked me to hide under the bed. Confused, I nevertheless did as told. Within minutes we heard the heavy footsteps of Dr. Popper and then a hard knock at the door. Eva opened the door, and Dr. Popper stormed into the room, turned on all the lights, examined every corner of the room, and then slowly moved toward the bed. My heart froze. I inched back toward the wall and covered my face with my hands. "Please God," I prayed, "make me invisible." When she peered under the bed, she couldn't see me. The shadows must have been deep and dark enough to hide my slender, black-clothed body . . . or God had answered my prayer.

Then I heard her explain to Eva that nobody in the big house knew where I had gone, and my sister told them I liked to take a walk after dinner. She continued, "I thought I saw the silhouette of two figures in your room just before you turned off the light after I called you." Her voice was stern and hard. "Do you know where Dagmar is?"

"Well, you've seen for yourself that she does not seem to be here," Eva lied in a surprisingly defiant tone.

"Very well. If you see her let us know." Dr. Popper left the room and rushed down the steps and back toward the main house.

I had never felt more guilty and more relieved than the moment I heard the door shut behind her. I did not then understand her anger, nor did I understand Eva's desire to hide me from her. I came out from under the bed, gave Eva a quick hug, opened the door carefully, and fled. I slipped down the steps as quietly as possible and stepped out into a night illuminated only by the crescent of the moon and a lone star. For a moment I stood still and thanked God for the miracle of escaping some unknown, but clearly insidious, danger. Suddenly, a bright flashlight shone into my face. I could see nothing and no one.

A voice shrieked at me, "So, you were with her after all! Shame on you!"

Shame for what? Taking a walk? Reading poetry? Then, slowly, something deep inside me began to melt, and hot tears rushed to my eyes. I began to shake and sob uncontrollably and inconsolably. When I look back at that moment, I realize that what welled up from within me was more than fear of exposure to some unknown accusation; it was deep sorrow for the loss of innocence and fury at the injustice of it all.

Both my sister and I were expelled—or maybe I was expelled and Utzi chose to leave too; I don't remember. And, of course, Eva lost her job. It was years later before I understood that we must have been presumed to be lesbian lovers. Eva and I remained friends for many years. For a while she was engaged to an American she'd met when she came to the United States on a Fulbright scholarship; but she later married Peter, an Austrian, and had four or five children. Then I lost track of her.

Years later she discovered my whereabouts, and the last I heard from her was of her husband's death. In her note, she described how horribly difficult it had been to take care of someone with brain cancer and how frightening the future was that loomed before her now. I remember how in love they had been and a love scene I had once witnessed. To a fifteen-year-old, it was fascinating to watch Peter's hands move along Eva's shoulders and down her spine, and her hand on his knee and her eyes distant, dreamy. Peter turned to me and said, "You don't mind, do you?" He then took her in his arms, and for the first time in my life I saw a man and woman kiss. The kiss seemed to go on forever. I was a bit uneasy at first but kept watching, trance-like. I thought then how beautiful love must be and wished that one day I, too, would have such passion in my life.

I know that this innocent love for Eva in my early teens opened my mind and heart to understand and value later in life all kinds of love. In the late seventies, when homophobia was rampant in the women's movement, I never feared or despised my lesbian sisters, because a long time ago I had learned to appreciate women's love for women.

Many years later, in the waning days of my years as First Lady of Ohio, Stonewall Union, a political action group committed to fighting for the civil rights of gay people, decided to honor both Dick and me for the work we had done in defense of Ohio's gay community. Only I was able to attend the event in Cincinnati, and I knew that this was a speech I needed to prepare for. I spent considerable time formulating my remarks and decided to use the occasion of accepting the joint award to affirm the validity and goodness at the heart of all love. In my remarks I wanted to pay homage to all kinds of love and to those who struggle against the odds to make the world a safer place for all lovers. I received a standing ovation, and scores of people stopped by after the event to thank me for my courage and the clarity of my vision. But that moment of hope and honor was dashed weeks later when a reporter for the *Cleveland Plain Dealer,* using an obscure gay newspaper as her "source," delighted in announcing to the world her own conclusion that the First Lady of Ohio had come out of the closet. *No need for that,* I thought in reading the vicious column. *I came out from under the bed years ago!*

I have loved much, and I never want to lose my passion for celebrating the diversity of people, places, and things around me. I am not simply straight or gay, lesbian or bisexual—or any other label society assigns. The kind of love I affirm is more than the freedom to share bodies gently and generously. True love is about empathy, compassion, and forgiveness. True love is patient, kind, and yet seldom pure and requires all of us—straight or gay or celibate, abandoned or adored, sober or addicted—to continue the struggle to lovingly overcome greed, envy, ego, jealousy, and resentment.

For as far back as my memory takes me, it has been mostly women who brought security and nourishment into my life, loving me unconditionally and helping me maintain perspective and balance. The ability to achieve balance is connected to the inner ear; remembering and listening to our past is what moves yet protects us. The dangerous balancing act of life thus requires a kind of perfect pitch. Listening to women's voices has taught me to hear my own; following their lead has helped me to center myself and become a leader. Together, we have learned to break the silence, cushioned each other's falls, recorded our lives, remembered our pain, reclaimed our power, recovered our sanity.

Doris Bernatzik, Ilse Leschanovsky, and I became fast friends when I transferred to Billroth Schule. Up until that time, I had had a number of girlfriends but no best friend. (Maybe Utzi had been my best friend. She certainly was my most steady playmate throughout my childhood.) For the next ten years, Doris was my best friend. She was taller than I, better looking, and blonde, and she got better grades. Because her family had social status, her manners were polished; even our professors were in awe of her. Most of the time I felt inadequate around her, but I also felt challenged and stretched beyond my own world. She was a fine writer and to this day is one of those authors who can captivate a reader's imagination and focus their attention.

Doris developed her own style very early. Her walk was uninhibited, and her nearsightedness gave her a somewhat mysterious look, making it possible for her to get away with acknowledging only those people who interested her. Her manner of speech was all her own, too. She combined High German with bits of Viennese dialect and had a deep appreciation for the unique and beautiful in language. She introduced me to the poet Rainer Maria Rilke. From Doris I learned to love my own mother tongue, and through her I became curious about the transformative power of words.

The rose garden at the back of her house was a constant source of delight and amusement to us. We would name the beautiful roses after people we liked and the wilted, tired-looking ones after people we despised. It was more than a game. Doris taught me the power inherent in using my senses to name my reality. To this day, she is a very sensuous woman, and I realize another of her special gifts to me was showing me how to savor life's many sensual surprises. Together we climbed the cherry trees and gorged ourselves on the ripest fruit. There were three kinds of cherry trees in her front yard: firm white heart cherries, bright-red sour cherries, and deep-red Moorkirschen. We mused at length over the merits of cherries versus strawberries and agreed that there was something almost subversive about the soft hairiness of raspberries, especially when served with sour cream. While we chose to eat strawberries straight from the strawberry patch, when it came to red currants and rhubarb we took pleasure in sitting down at a table bedecked with Hoffman china and silver to eat bowls of fruit with powdered sugar accompanied by fresh black bread slathered with unsalted butter and Brie.

The Bernatzik family was very cosmopolitan, and their house was always full of interesting guests from all over the world. Doris taught me to surround myself with living art in the intimate sphere of my own home rather than just worship artists from afar and in museums. Her home was an exquisite expression of fin-de-siècle sensibilities. Built by the famous Viennese architect Joseph Hoffman and furnished by the Wiener Werkstaette (the Viennese Arts and Crafts Association), the house—everything from the doorknobs to the utensils—was custom designed. The living room was painted in a soft flesh tone, and one whole wall had floor-to-ceiling shelves displaying African art objects behind glass doors. On the opposite wall were large windows, and over the piano hung a large Gustav Klimt painting entitled *Hope II*. The painting represented a pregnant woman and her female friends, with an almost transparent ivory skeleton just barely visible in the opulent gold of her ceremonial gown. Above the living room couch was an equally large original painting by Egon Schiele that depicted houses clustered along the banks of a nearly black river. The contrast between the two paintings was striking. The Klimt was almost transparent, sensual, in its golds and mauves and exuded hope and life. In contrast, Schiele's wild, dark, menacing currents conjured feelings of fear and despair.

A built-in music system and the most spectacular collection of classical music completed the environment that was so different from my own middle-class surroundings. We did have books, some original art, and a record player, but it was all very modest and conventional. I envied Doris her life. (Only years later did she confess to me that she had envied me my mother, because Mutti clearly cared about and fussed over me and, unlike her own mother, was friendly and unpretentious.) That world became my secret standard by which to measure "the good life"; to this day, the perfect house is that Hoffman home just outside the Vienna woods, on Springsiedelgasse.

It was a happy coincidence that the Ohio Governor's Residence also had a strong Arts and Crafts flavor. The house had been designed according to the principles of the English movement exemplified by the Scottish architect Charles Mackintosh, who was the original inspiration for Joseph Hoffman. Thanks to our friend Alicia Miller and architect Steve Bucchieri, we were able to redecorate the house based on those principles. Steve designed furniture that incorporated the grids represented throughout the Residence in windows, wall paneling, and slate floors. We brought together a handful of indigenous Ohio craftspeople and created a furniture business association on Murray Hill in Cleveland to produce furnishings for the Governor's Residence. Our respect for the integrity of the architecture and empowering of local craftspeople was very different from how other official residences around the country had been restored; in many other states, millions of dollars had been raised and then spent on costly antiques from around the world or, worst yet, on reproductions of originals.

Doris introduced me to simplicity as well as extravagance. She shared with me the music of Bach, perfect Christmas trees, and long walks in the middle of the night. We spent many hours walking her dog, Assra, talking about friendship, men, art, and the difficulties of composing one's life like a piece of art. Like Eva before her, Doris struck some deep, responsive chord in me and helped me develop confidence and self-esteem. She believed in me when others, especially my teachers, found little to praise. She helped me survive my parents' incessant battles and was there to lift me out of depression after my sister's death. She taught me about the healing power of music. Together we joined the Jeunesse Musicale Choir and worked diligently to master Mozart, Hayden, Honegger, and much more, and we spent many hours listening to the emerging new talents of the day—Von Karajan, Maazel, and others. Since we never had to grow old together, live with each other, fight over men, or compete in any other way, our affection for one other continued, uncontaminated by reality. We made the simple promise that we would be friends always.

But my true best female friend was my own sister, Utzi. Much of my search for sisterhood over the years has its roots in that deep and almost magic early childhood connection. Death did not rob me of Utzi. She continues to be at my side—in the sounds of Elvis and the blues, in the light of blue moons, in the quest for blue roses. She continues to inspire and guide.

4

"Lately I've been thinking about Ohio
Thinking what Ohio means to me"

Hope is the thing with feathers
that perches in the soul.
—*Emily Dickinson*

Cleveland, Ohio
October 18, 1995
Feast of Saint Luke (patron saint of artists)
This fall in Ohio I see red—the rich russet of the foliage and the crimson hues of a sunrise, cheeks flushed from excitement and eyes sore and swollen from tears of sorrow. And cardinals.

Whenever I see a cardinal, I recall the grief of a friend who lost her son to suicide. She told me that the day after the funeral, she was deeply depressed and hardly able to do simple daily chores—until she noticed a cardinal following her from room to room. Wherever she went he was there outside the window, just beyond reach but visible and bright. Her son had been a Worthington High School Cardinal, and she felt certain that he had sent her this feathered messenger to console her and to assure her that he was okay. I also recall the spring of my mother-in-law's dying. The days were sunny and warm, and cardinals came to visit her daily, even knocking on the windows. Could she see them? Could she hear their song? Did they bring her comforting messages from the world beyond the limits of her deathbed? In some ancient and indigenous traditions, birds were often thought to be messengers from beyond.

"There is a fierce kind of beauty in dying. Death and beauty are two exalted realities filled with equal amounts of shadow and light," Victor Hugo wrote, comparing them to "two sisters, frightening and fruitful, puzzle and certainty at the same time."

My deepest hope is that in the end all is well. Despite the fact that our own bodies will seem to betray us and the best of friends will appear to have abandoned us, there might be, beyond the reach of death, a silent flame of true love braving even the deepest darkness of despair and grief. My simple wish is perhaps best expressed by a few beautifully crafted lines written by the Austrian poet Ingeborg Bachmann:

Bei dir sein moechte ich bis ans Ende aller Tage und auf den Grund dieses Abgrundes in den ich stuerze mit dir. Ich moechte ein Ende mit dir, ein Ende. Und eine Revolte gegen das Ende der Liebe in jeden Augenblick und bis zum Ende.

To be with you until the end of all days, that I desire. And together to reach the bottom of this descent. I want an end with you in the end. And every moment—from now until then— a revolt against the end of love until the end.[1]

My sister's nickname was Vogi, which means baby bird. Her simple grave has a natural rock surrounded by an arch of bronze roses, and perched on one of the thorny twigs is a small sparrow. Some people think that our souls return to the stars; some believe we dissolve into energy; some hope there is a parallel universe where we will find again all those we love. I suspect some special souls might choose to return to earth as these feathered, light-winged creatures to help us grow hope—not only for safe passage home after death but hope in the possibility of our winging toward a grand homecoming on earth right here and now.

One of my favorite places in the Governor's Residence was the small living room in the back of the house. There I could sit by a warm fire and watch all sorts of birds, especially cardinals, come and go from our many feeders. Maybe tomorrow, on my way home, I will drive by that lovely house on the corner of Parkview and Maryland and thank God once again for the wonder-filled time our family spent there together and the miracle of us alive and of our story still unfolding. I trust I will spot a few of my

---

1. Ingeborg Bachmann, *Songs in Flight: The Collected Poems of Ingeborg Bachmann*, trans. Paul Filkins (Marsilio, 1995).

feathered friends and possibly even catch a glimpse of the garden ready for harvest. Maybe then I can recover just enough courage to soften my hardened heart and ready it once again for love and splendor beyond grief.

U tzi died when I was fifteen years old. I will never forget the shrill ring of the telephone call that brought us the devastating news. Mutti's face exploded in terror at the first words of the simple sentence: "Frau Doktor Braun, there has been a serious accident. Your husband is out of danger, but your daughter is in critical condition."

Both Vati and Utzi had been taken to Hanusch Hospital on the other side of Vienna. I don't remember who drove us to the hospital, but I do remember praying incessantly, "Please God, don't let her die." We rushed into the hospital, and the few seconds it took to give our name to the receptionist were enough for me to pick up the piercing cry of what sounded like a child some distance away down the hall. That was the last time I heard my sister's voice.

We were first taken to see my father. He was in pain but alive and out of danger. He had a few broken ribs and was concerned about reassuring my mother that from now on all would be well. Things would be different. He would change. He needed her forgiveness. He promised to make love to her again, to have more babies—anything to move beyond the terror of the unfolding disaster. We all wanted to believe that there still was time and hope for us as a family and that Utzi would survive. Then Mutti and I rushed to Utzi's bedside. A brain injury had rendered her unconscious.

On the way back from a funeral service for a friend, my father's sky-blue Volkswagen skidded on an ice patch and smashed into a telegraph post. The post broke in half, and the top portion crashed onto the roof of the car, hitting exactly where Utzi was sitting, crushing her skull. Strangely, nothing else was broken, or even damaged; even the glass brandy flask in the glove compartment remained intact, and the car was able to be driven away from the scene.

45

When I first saw Utzi, she hardly seemed different, and hope quickened in my heart. But in no time convulsions ravaged her whole body and the bitter truth began to sink in. "Hopeless. There is nothing we can do for her, Frau Doktor," I heard the young intern whisper to my mother. They kept assuring us that she did not feel anything. "How do they know that?" I thought to myself, and something inside me began to rage. Utzi fought hard. Her young body was strong and healthy and not at all ready to relinquish life. I wanted to believe a miracle would happen.

Sometime during our vigil, the young doctor returned. He sat at her bedside and quietly cried. That's when I realized all hope was gone. Her feet and arms turned inward, her heartbeat slowed down, and then she was gone. Mutti said she felt her spirit leaving and saw the door open and softly close again. They say souls sometimes leave that way. I felt abandoned.

Many years later when Natalie, our youngest daughter, hovered between life and death, Dick had a similar experience. I had spent the previous night and all day at the hospital with Natalie after finally convincing the doctors to operate for appendicitis. They did not believe appendicitis could be the problem in an eighteen-month-old baby. But appendicitis it was, and by the time they opened her up forty-eight hours later, it had ruptured. When I left the hospital that day, exhausted, Dick took over the night watch. Sometime during the night, he felt the door opening and someone entering the room. Natalie opened her eyes and Dick managed to hold her gaze, eye to eye, and eventually she smiled at him and went back to sleep. Surviving that night was crucial for her recovery, and to this day Dick believes that had he not been there to catch her gaze, she would have left with whoever it was who had entered the room. Dick believes it was Death he managed to outwit that night. I choose to believe that the little sister who mysteriously slipped away that December night in Hanusch Hospital returned to help Natalie. I choose to believe that Utzi has become our family's guardian spirit.

46

Mutti took Utzi's death very hard and very personally. Up until then, she had felt close to God and raised us to trust in Him. But now she held God responsible for the absurdity, the randomness of Utzi's death. She had struggled to protect us from bombs and to scrape together an existence out of nothing all those years only to have her daughter wasted in a senseless car crash. She felt betrayed by God and my father and, except for my wedding, didn't step inside a church again until years later when her grandchildren came to stay with her in Vienna. It took almost a decade for her grief to soften, and this truce between her and her God is still an uneasy one. She lost faith—not so much in God's ability but in His willingness to protect her children, to intervene on their behalf when it counts most.

To this day, Mutti believes that what mothers don't do for their children no one else will. In her mind, to be a good mother is to be available to your daughter—always. Even now, she will try to influence me but never holds it against me if I reject her advice and choose my own way. And though we have long been separated by half a world, I can count on her daily rosary blessing. Indeed, despite the great distance, she has managed to be at my side whenever there was a crisis in my life. For many years I resented her fierce loyalty and relentless giving. I felt unable to respond in kind. It was too demanding. But I've come to realize that this is just her way of loving and living and that there are no strings attached to her generosity of heart and spirit. Faithfulness to those she loves is the lesson she came to learn and teach.

Not long before my sister died, my parents had decided to get a divorce. My sister never accepted their decision, and the night before the accident she told me, "You watch and see! I will figure out a way to keep them together." The tragedy of her sudden death stopped the divorce proceedings, and my parents reconciled just as she had predicted. Utzi's deepest wish came true.

I don't think I truly forgave my father for my sister's death until a few months before his own. I had let go of my desire to be loved by him many years before. I had detached myself from his angry outbursts and irrational behaviors. I had forgiven him for all he could not be for me. But it was only a few weeks before his death that I came to realize that I had buried almost beyond retrieval a hatred so subtle it contaminated much of my consciousness and continued to confound my conscience.

I spent much time in prayer asking my God to free my heart from this festering fury. Finally, I decided to send a telegram and tell him that I loved him. I discovered I could not do it in German without feeling like a fraud, and I knew I could not do it in English without offending him; so I chose to write in Italian, a language we both shared and loved. My mother told me that he kept that message close to him until the end. He died without ever telling any of us that he loved us and without ever being able to show his wife of more than fifty years appreciation and gratitude for her loyalty and dedicated care.

The many battles between my parents, combined with the sudden trauma of Utzi's death, took their toll. My grades suffered, and I had to repeat that whole school year. This failure almost crushed my already badly bruised self-esteem. Being sent to a new school to make up the year meant loss of face, loss of friends, loss of confidence. And to complete the depressing scene, I lost my boyfriend that summer to some rich blonde willing to have sex. In retrospect, however, that difficult winter became one of my greatest blessings, for my new school, Neuland, was in every sense "new land" for me.

For years I had been taught a severe, narrow, moralizing, Protestant-bashing type of Catholicism in public schools. But Neuland was different. It was a Catholic Institute founded by a group of women who wanted to create a religious teaching order for women interested in instructing girls from all classes and denominations. Rather than habits, they wore sensible clothes and simple hairstyles. Predictably, the Vatican refused to support them; but, undeterred, they persevered anyway, without official approval. They raised enough money to build a school and proceeded to design a curriculum that not only was accredited by the Austrian Ministry of Education but also offered much beyond academic excellence. Believing in diversity, Neuland was open to students of different backgrounds, abilities, and, most important, religions. The school's administrators and educators used those differences to open our young, impressionable minds to other perspectives and to teach tolerance and love.

Even though my best friend, Doris, was a Lutheran, as were two of my three cousins, I knew very little about Protestants or Jews before I went to Neuland. There we had to periodically attend a religion class other than our own and simply listen. The professors at Neuland were extraordinary (most, if not all, our professors were qualified to teach at the university), and their commitment to the students was exceptional. In contrast to public school, at Neuland teachers and pupils were on a first-name basis, and the friendly, personal tenor encouraged a true spirit of partnership between students and professors. We had to attend Mass once during the week and, of course, were expected to celebrate Sunday Eucharist. We were offered the opportunity for confession weekly but were not pushed to go. These women really cared not just about our minds and our bodies but about our souls as well. Josepha Grois, our educator, would spend whole afternoons tutoring us for upcoming examinations, and Grete Hoffa, our science and math professor, was always available for additional explanations of the finer points of algebra and trigonometry.

The most extraordinary teacher was Lotte Leitmeier, who taught us English, Latin, and theology. She also taught canon law at the University of Vienna; at the time, she was the only female canon lawyer in the world. The law students, especially the men, considered her fierce and distant, but to us young women she was a wonderful mentor. She had been on a lecture tour in the United States and greatly admired the practical faith of American Catholics. She marveled at the fact that so many voluntarily contributed close to 10 percent of their income to their church. In Austria, the bishops chose to keep the church tax instituted by Hitler, because without law-threatening punishment Austrian Catholics would just drop their pennies in the basket on Sunday and live off the generosity of the Vatican, which, in turn, lived off the largesse of American Catholics.

There was nothing easy about Lotte Leitmeier. Her features were almost coarse, certainly severe. Her voice was deep and her hands strong. She had black hair, dark eyes, terrible posture, and wore not a trace of makeup, ever. She had a mighty stride and a way of speech that cut right through all pretense. She could look straight into the depths of one's soul. During Mass she almost never did the expected—she knelt when she felt like it, stayed seated when everyone else was standing, and most of the time had her elbows on her knees and her head buried in the palms of her hands. Although she prayed with us out loud, she almost never sang along. Sometimes her eyes betrayed her; she appeared to be in some sort of physical pain much of the time, and something inside her soul seemed locked in combat with unknown forces. Her irreverence toward clerics was matched only by her love for the church as a community of believers. She was a credible, practical mystic. She taught us to trust our inner voice and to be true to our own conscience. She demanded disciplined performance in her class, and it never occurred to us not to give it to her.

I fell in love with Lotte the first time I saw her. I would have done anything for her, and under her firm guidance I, who could not even pass Latin the year before, began to excel in that and all her other subjects. Theology had been an easy, throwaway course all through secondary school, until Lotte made it difficult and significant for me. She taught religion hand in hand with philosophy, psychology, and church history. Her approach was not only interdisciplinary and cross-cultural but also fascinating and even fun. Her enthusiasm for all things healthy and holy was infectious. She loved to hike and garden, and she almost always had a large sheepdog at her side. Learning with Lotte taught me that searching for divine truths is an essential quest and one of life's greatest adventures. She exuded a fiery passion that made everything bright and alive. In a way, she was quite subversive and counterpatriarchal. Many years later, when I introduced my husband to her, she played the role of an interesting, aging academic—a bit eccentric, with a good sense of humor, but quite harmless.

She was, however, anything but safe. She demanded the will to goodness—even heroic greatness—from those who chose to enter her mystic maze. To have a teacher who lives what she preaches is a great blessing, and to have known Dr. Lotte Leitmeier was to be called to follow her. But following her was not some dependent, weak-spined act. It meant embracing and connecting with everything that was warm and sparkling and being ready to break into a wild dance.

Lotte was the original feminist in my life: a woman who could measure up in a man's world but chose women and girls as her confidantes and companions. I heard rumors that the Russians raped her when they liberated Bisamberg, her hometown, and that she never cared to marry after that. Who knows? She never discussed it with her students, and the few times I have been with her since I graduated from Neuland have not lent themselves to intimate inquiry into her past or why she chose not to marry. She was my first real spiritual guide, and I wish I had lived closer to her to continue learning from her.

It was Lotte who encouraged me to go to Oxford, England, and who one day mentioned in passing that her favorite saint was Teresa of Avila. I decided to investigate why and discovered in Carmelite saints a spiritual well that has continued to refresh my life. Since then, I've tried to learn everything possible about those other doctors of the church. In the late 1980s I joined the board of an organization called Mary's Pence (in contrast to Peter's Pence), a Catholic women's foundation dedicated to the empowerment of women. The foundation raises money for Catholic women working with poor women throughout the Americas. It is no coincidence that Mary's Pence Day is celebrated annually on October 15, which happens to be Teresa of Avila's feast day. Mary's Pence is an effort by feminist Catholic women to transform anger about the church's neglect of women into positive action and to participate in recovering *our* Church by empowering those women in need of help and healing.

When I was about fifteen I began to feel frustration with my Church—not with God or Jesus and Mary, not with Christians or even ordinary Catholics, just with that proud and patriarchal institution. I resented the arrogance of some of their pronouncements, the blatant discrimination against girls and women, and the unrepented crimes throughout history, like the inquisitions and the witch hunts. I cannot remember the specific reason for my sudden rebellion. Perhaps they had refused someone Communion or a proper burial, or maybe I was disappointed in how little attention they had paid to my sister's real life at her funeral and my mother's real needs after my sister's death. I really can't remember. What I do remember is the day I stepped up to Lotte's desk after class and announced to her that I was leaving the Church. Barely looking up from her papers, she just slightly adjusted her glasses and gave me one of her amused sideways glances and kept on correcting the papers in front of her. I stood there amazed that a religion teacher could care so little whether or not I left the Church.

Finally, she did look up and said, "Can I help you somehow?"

"Well, yes," I mumbled. "How does one go about checking out officially?"

"Oh, that's simple enough," came her reply. "Just go to your parish church and reclaim your baptism certificate."

"Then what?" I asked.

"Well, then rip it up or burn it or frame it or whatever," she said.

I was speechless. I expected anger, sadness, anything but acceptance. Lotte went back to work on her papers, and it was clear that the conversation was over. But then, just as I was about to close the door behind me, she gently called my name. "Dagmar," she said. "Remember, never slam a door shut without opening a window."

After that exchange I never bothered to leave the Church. I've shut many a door and have had a few slammed in my face, but so far the slightly open windows of Vatican II have provided me with enough fresh air to continue my faith journey under the protective mantle of Mother Church.

I don't remember whose idea the pilgrimage was. Certainly not mine. Even though the spiritual focus of Neuland was the Risen Christ, not Marian piety, all but a handful of us decided that if we passed our oral and written final exam (Matura), we would forfeit our fancy class trip to Italy and instead walk to Maria Zell, a famous Austrian shrine dedicated to the Mother of God. To this day, many Austrians believe that prayers to Mary caused the miracle of Austrian liberation from foreign occupation after 1945. Why not? And there are just as many now, including Pope John Paul II, who believe it was Mary's intervention that helped break down communism throughout Europe. Again, why not? What I do know is that all of us did pass the Matura!

"I am glad to have it known
Ohio is my home"

Because it is not lasting, let us not fall into the cynic's trap and call it an illusion. Duration is not a test of true or false.
—*Anne Morrow Lindbergh*

Cleveland, Ohio
October 27 and 28, 1995
Today, on the eve of Dick's remarriage, my mind is in search of a way out.
Yet I know well that the only way out of grief is through it.

Over my lifetime I have been dislocated by war, politics, and, now, divorce. I know how to recover and reorient; I know I will in time even transform my family and overcome homesickness once again. But no matter how long I live, I will never forget the gut-wrenching pain of this night. Loss is loss is loss. Losing my spouse to divorce and remarriage feels worse than relinquishing him to an untimely death.

Early this morning I began to rework chapter 5, only to discover that it is crammed full of courtship and romance memories, full of recollections of our wedding and honeymoon, leave-taking and homemaking. How could I possibly work my way through this today? But then I realized that perhaps the retelling of how this star-crossed love story began, what happened along the way, and how it ended is one way of helping me survive the next twenty-four hours and beyond.

I can't help but wonder . . . . How many of our friends will show up at this wedding? Will they be celebrating, or just gawking? Will anyone object? How many of our children will feel obliged to attend?

I'm told that the other side of sorrow is anger. Tonight I can feel the heat of my anger like never before, taste my bitterness; I can feel myself reverberate with restorative rage, and I know that to deny anger is to short-circuit healing. And so I continue to move through the scorching, purifying fire of all stages

57

of grieving, beginning with the stun of shock and comfort of denial, past the futility of bargaining, and finally through anger to acceptance, to peace.

Some well-meaning folks try to comfort me by promising that what goes around comes around. Perhaps. But I find no comfort in wishing misfortune on the one I love. Besides, I've noticed that those in power rarely suffer the consequences of their actions . . . at least not in this lifetime. Moreover, those with the power to inflict pain and injustice also find ways to project their confusions, prejudices, contradictions, and especially their guilty consciences on fellow travelers, innocent bystanders, whole communities, and inevitably their own families. Nevertheless, it is also true that all of us have all the power to manifest our heart's deepest desires, to attain our wishes and dreams. However, with dreams as touchstones to our souls, we need to be careful to remember and reflect on our dreams once we awake and to discipline and tame the more destructive desires they project. We cannot make our own dreams come true by reducing the lives of others to nightmares.

To move beyond the anger, the rage, I need to reclaim a wholesome freedom, the gospel freedom that is about justice and true love, what theologian Rebecca Chopp calls "emancipatory transformation."[1] Some have proclaimed there is no peace without justice and that there can be no justice without forgiveness. If we agree to that much, we come to see that there also can be no forgiveness without honest repentance.

· · ·

A few years ago, Mary Jo Ruggieri and I helped Ann Castle, the founder of the Inn at Cedar Falls, negotiate her final passage. The Inn, located in Logan, Ohio, began in 1985 as the vision of this extraordinary woman. Together with a small cluster of friends, she converted an old cabin into an inn where people could retreat to a simpler way of life, reconnect with nature, and experience deep-breathing space for their souls and spirits. Her circle of friends and believers widens every year, and Ann's dream of providing a place of hospitality to those in search of natural soul food lives on.

---

1. Rebecca Chopp, *Saving Work: Feminist Practices of Theological Education* (Westminster John Knox, 1997).

The first time I met Ann was after our last Willaloo gathering. I decided to take Dick and a half-dozen others to lunch at the nearby Inn. Ann was pleased to welcome the governor to her place but spent little time with him. She did not attempt to flatter him or me. She seemed tired, distracted, anxious. After we finished lunch, she pulled me aside and told me, in an almost conspiratorial way, to take time out from all the hustle and bustle and learn to celebrate myself. "When you turn fifty," she said, "you have to change your pace and, most important of all, take time to recover your own dream."

I didn't know then that her own time was running out rapidly, that her cancer had returned. I didn't dream then that before I would celebrate my fifty-third birthday my own life, as I knew and loved it, would be shattered. And I had no way of knowing then that the lessons I came to learn from this dying woman would help me to accept and appreciate the honor of helping to care for my dying mother-in-law, to prepare me for my own father's death, and to cope with the unexpected implosion of our marriage— all in the same year.

Ann's lesson harmonized with that of another spiritual guide who re-entered my life today, on Dick's second wedding day. Initially I thought I would leave town for the day, maybe travel to Toronto to see The Phantom of the Opera. *Instead, I spent this morning at the Ursuline motherhouse, where feminist author Sister Madonna Kolbenschlag was leading a retreat entitled "A Woman's Way." I joined other women in exploring the growing phenomenon of women's spirituality as a force for change and as the impetus of the human healing agenda. In this, my darkest hour, Madonna helped me discover what good was hidden in the shadows.*

When Madonna asked us to recreate our life's time line, highlighting the most significant transitions, I could hardly do the exercise. I was flooded by the intense memory of doing this very exercise with Dick in one of our many marriage retreats. Only then we were asked to imagine extending our time line to our death day and to place on it our hopes for the rest of our lives as well as our best memories so far. Back then, the desire to be together to the end of our days was the most cherished hope for us both. To see our grandchildren and great-grandchildren born and grow, to be there for each other even beyond death itself was the promise we renewed that day. And now here I was, alone, working my way down the same lifeline, marking all those passages again and wondering if at the very moment I jotted down August 24, 1962, he might not be making the same promises to another that he once made to me.

In *"Getting Back to Kansas," the final chapter in* Lost in the Land of Oz, *Madonna Kolbenschlag writes,*

Our universe is neither random, nor finished, nor progressive—it is simply growing. We are like a fetal organism, connected to and suspended in Gaia, waiting in darkness for the advent of a new birth, so now you are back in Kansas. By comparison with Oz, it seems a bit drab, gray, and dull. But at least it is real. You are conscious of having left your companions behind, it was a tearful good-bye, and it will be a permanent loss. What now? Everything is less than it should be, but now you have a better idea why. You have a better idea of what had been missing in yourself, in your work, in your living situation, in your relationships, in your action, in your world. At long last you are befriending your inner orphan. Now that you've been there you can map the journey. You will need the map because the journey sometimes goes in circles. If you've been there before, you will probably find yourself there again— but with a difference: You will see the way ahead more clearly through the mist: You will recognize your own footprints leading back from Oz.²

As I explored my most memorable transitions, I came to see the points of arrival and departure of my various journeys. The first journey, out of childhood, helped me end the dysfunctional dance of father- and mother-worship. But I realized that I continued to practice with everyone I have ever loved the waltz steps I learned from them. My second journey taught me to leave home and along the way learn to weave a web of solidarity with others in search of a safe space. Slowly I began to overcome my fear of survival in this ever-changing world. The third journey is into aging and death,

2. Madonna Kolbenschlag, *Lost in the Land of Oz: Befriending Your Inner Orphan and Heading for Home* (Crossroad, 1994).

which, in contrast to love, is the uninvited but ever-faithful companion. I've come to understand that death is not a private matter; just as we are born into the strong hands of another living person, so, too, do we die in the gentle arms of those who have moved on to another life, one beyond deadlines and time lines. We are neither born alone nor die alone. I realized today that death and divorce emerge as the themes of my most passion-filled passages. While my sister's death seemed to prevent our parents' looming divorce, the deaths of my mother-in-law and father seemed to almost facilitate Dick's decision to leave.

. . .

After the retreat, I headed for Columbus . . . and my children. When I arrived at Christopher and Melanie's house, Gabriella, my oldest daughter, was playing with my grandchildren, Eleanor, Max, and Julia, while Chris and Melanie, their parents, were preparing the family meal. I watched them with tremendous pride. All of this family upheaval motivated them to work even harder at their own relationship.

I could not sleep that night. I could not stop crying. Sometime during the night, Christopher came downstairs, and we just sat in the dark holding each other while deep waves of sorrow washed over me. I remembered my mother's words, "It's good to cry; it calms the nerves"; and those of Teresa of Avila, "Tears are what waters the garden of the soul." I prayed in silence for my tears to cleanse me so that one day soon I could once more be my hopeful, cheerful self. But this night there was no hope. The darkness was total. There was only the even breathing of my son holding me close.

After returning from the pilgrimage to Maria Zell, I dedicated myself to virginity and motherhood. I decided that I wanted to remain a virgin always—but in more than the conventional sense of reserving full sexual consummation for life consecrated in marriage. It was less because I feared pregnancy or even God than because I wanted to feel "free" to conceive a child the first time I made love to a man. While I decided to wait until my honeymoon to experience full sexual union, I freely indulged in sensual intimacies before marriage, and with more than one man. I believed then and now that sex at its best is essentially an exploration of joy and other intrinsically spiritual realms, such as creativity. In my own marriage, our best sexual experiences resulted in pregnancies. We certainly did not intend to create a child every time we made love, but every time we did conceive we knew it from the special intensity and sweetness of the lovemaking.

Indeed, lovemaking free of fear or compulsion can make our spirit soar to great heights and let our soul revel in pure joy. And yet sex can also be used to undermine, dominate, and imprison one's own or another's body, mind, and soul. I have come to see it as my duty to reject the Vatican's excessive claim of dominion over my conscience and to resist her often perverse invasions into my most private spheres. When she insists on probing and invading our souls against our will, she is guilty of spiritual battery. When she denies men and women the basic human right to choose their own way of lovemaking according to their own conscience, she distorts the goodness of Jesus Christ, who lived and died to free us for loving.

It may have been Ulli, my best friend at Neuland, who introduced me to Lajos Ruff at a party in Vienna in about 1957. He was in his early thirties, a Hungarian, a writer, and nothing at all like the rest of my friends. He was more experienced in life and lovemaking than anyone I had ever met. To my consternation, he invited me to come to his apartment on our first date. When I accepted, as he later told me, he was quite surprised. In the 1950s, young Viennese women seldom took that kind of a chance; we were regularly warned about the cunning nature of men who lured innocent girls into their bachelor dens only to ravish and ruin them.

Certainly, I was more than a bit naive. I was sixteen and full of idealism, especially about freedom and love. Why did I choose to trust this complete stranger? I had heard some wild stories about his sexual appetites and his skill in pleasing women. Maybe I was curious to experience more than I was willing to admit. Or perhaps I was flattered by the attention of an attractive older man and wanted to appear to be sophisticated. I think at heart, however, it was less my trust in him than my trust in myself that made me brave and fearless. I wanted to affirm that women are free to stand by their desires, capable of discerning how far is far enough, and entitled to expect that men stop their advances when told to do so.

His mother lived with him in his flat, and I was relieved when I learned that she was home that night (I thought it less likely that a man would rape a woman right next door to his mother's bedroom). Lajos served me a brandy, and we settled down in his very large and comfortable living room. We spent the rest of the evening listening to music, discussing literature and politics, and slowly getting to know each other. He did not kiss me (not until our second or third date) and made a point of allowing me to get home by my curfew. Despite all the stories I had heard about this man's impatience with slow women, with me he seemed to pursue a different path. Much later in our relationship, he told me that the trust I put in him and the self-confidence I displayed that first evening touched him. He decided that very night that he wanted to spend the rest of his life with me, so he could take all the time necessary to set the stage for the first dance, the first kiss, the first trip out of town, the first night together, and many other firsts.

From the start Lajos accepted my desire to remain a virgin until my wedding night. That did not preclude wonderous sexual pleasuring. And his ability to eroticize even the smallest events—like slowly feeding me soft-boiled eggs on carefully buttered fresh bread—was stunning. Lajos helped me experience the connection between lust and pure joy. Because of him, I came to demand that my life be lived remembering that such elemental eroticism was not only possible but desirable and that it should not and could not be limited by rigid rules of church and state or even vows of marriage. While I believe that celibacy may facilitate priestly living and that monogamy may protect the integrity of the bond of marriage, I have come to realize that not all priests are truly called to celibacy, and I understand that not all spouses have a genuine call to monogamy. Therefore, the central challenge becomes not how to enforce celibacy and monogamy but how to balance and integrate the call to love and the desire to be free.

But deep inside I knew that my highest hopes and aspirations were not possible with Lajos. While he respected my desire to reserve intercourse for marriage, at the same time he also felt entitled to find from other women all I was still withholding from him. Late one morning I returned unexpectedly to his apartment to retrieve something I had forgotten. A very attractive woman in her late twenties was straightening out his room, making the bed Lajos and I had slept in for most of the previous night. Though friendly, she made it clear to me that, for the time being, she was the one who provided all Lajos really needed. "Maybe he admires your innocence enough to wait," she said, "but maybe not. In any event, he'll never be faithful to you, or to any other woman." I was not too surprised. I knew there were other women, and he had told me that sexual satisfaction was too important for him to do without. Still, everything changed that morning. Until then I thought I could accept infidelity as the inevitable consequence of my choice, my freedom, to abstain. My heart, still in love with romance, broke at hearing the simple truth of this woman's words, and my soul flew free to search for a love brave enough to resist temptations and delight in only us always.

My father never accepted Lajos. He was too old for me, and he was a foreigner. He thought that he would never finish his studies and that he was not a good enough writer to support a family. He even hired a detective to prove to me that bits and pieces of Lajos's life didn't match with the stories he had told me. Typically, however, the more Vati attempted to prove that Lajos was not the man to marry, the more I dug in my heels and invented reasons to stay in the relationship. But I had discovered much about Lajos myself. I'd come to realize that he made promises he did not keep. He promised to take me to my first ball. I was thrilled at the thought. Mutti bought me an expensive gown, matching shoes, and gloves. A few weeks before the event, it became clear that he had forgotten all about this promise.

Also, I discovered that I did not agree with his politics. Just as I was beginning to appreciate the more egalitarian views of social democrats in postwar Vienna, the very conservative Lajos surrounded himself with neo-monarchists. And I was deeply hurt that he never shared much of his writing with me.

After my Matura, my father offered to finance further studies anywhere but in Austria. He refused to grant me permission to marry, and since I was not yet twenty-one, I had to accept temporary defeat. And my mother reasoned that if this love for Lajos was real, a temporary separation could only strengthen it. So, after reviewing many options, I chose the Academy of English in Oxford, England, to prepare for the Cambridge Language Exams, which were necessary for study at any Oxford college. My plan was to be gone just long enough to turn twenty-one, to sit for the examination, and to return with a tangible certificate—and to Lajos. The last evening we spent together, Lajos gave me a marriage manual by Van de Felde and promised to wait—if not faithfully, nevertheless forever—and never marry anyone but me.

He kept his word. To this day, he remains unmarried, still living in Vienna. He once told me that I would always be his and would never find a man more capable of satisfying me. Back then I was bewildered by the intensity of his feelings and offended by his arrogance, but now I understand both better. He was the one who first helped me identify the connection between sexuality and spirituality. He was the first to adore both the sacred and profane in me. He also helped me see the importance of partnership in love, sex, marriage, birth, and work. But sometimes love is not enough. Even before I left for Oxford, I had begun to grow weary of Lajos's wild, bewildering ways.

I had known Peter Miculka, a friend from Jeunesse choir, for a few years before I chose to fall in love with him. I trusted this young man in a way I never trusted Lajos, or any man since, and he gave me the kind of security I missed and needed. Peter was simply a good man, and his singing voice manifested the strength and beauty of his soul. (As a young boy, he was a member of the Vienna Boys' Choir, where his natural talents were nurtured and appreciated.) After losing his father in the war, he had accepted the charge to stand by his widowed mother and take care of her always. Peter's tremendous integrity and commitment and his strong faith in God were most unusual and moving in someone so young.

Peter also had the most glorious body. Though we never fully consummated our relationship, we loved passionately and well. Peter wanted our relationship to last, always, but the timing was all wrong for me. While being together always felt right and good, I could not make a lasting commitment. I was in transition away from Lajos and toward England; I was searching for adventure and a way out of my family's pain and confusion. Sadly, Peter got lost in all that.

It was a short, intense romance with a wonderful Italian student at Oxford that finally freed me of Lajos's spell. Early in the term, Tancredi and I visited Stonehenge and watched the sun set over those mysterious, ancient boulders. I was overwhelmed with a sense of well-being and joy and felt called to consecrate my life to the pursuit of truth and love. I felt powerful and confident. That night in some small hotel room in London I initiated lovemaking for the first time. We still refrained from intercourse, but I felt a new, wild desire to please this man and make him feel wanted and powerful. For a few weeks, life and love seemed perfect. It ended when he left Oxford. He wanted me to come to Italy to meet his family, but, with my newfound strength and confidence, I had never felt freer and less interested in marrying. But my pre-Stonehenge self soon returned, and I regressed to my "normal" self, flirting furiously just for the fun of it and looking for a life partner rather than a life plan.

Then, on November 11, 1961, I was invited to a birthday party in honor of a young American named Dick Celeste. My Venezuelan friend Gina had been invited to the party by Michael Smyth, Dick's Australian roommate. Mike had charged the fun and friendly Gina with the responsibility of finding some nice girls from the Academy to liven up the surprise celebration for this Rhodes scholar from Ohio.

When Dick entered the living room that evening, I felt that the space was too small to contain his presence. He was full of life and mischief. He grabbed Gina, whirled her about, planted a big kiss on her forehead, and crashed into the nearest chair. In contrast to all the commotion his body brought into the room, his voice seemed to belong to someone different, someone calm, even shy. It was a most serious and sensual voice, strong and gentle and certainly very different from the high-pitched nasal tones of the British public-school types at the party.

He looked straight at me. I returned his gaze, smiled, and waited. Soon he got up and crossed the room. He tried to converse with me, but my ability to speak English was only slightly better than my comprehension of American idiom. (Of course, his German was nonexistent.) That night he walked me and Gina the few blocks down the street to our boardinghouse, clowning with Gina all the way. Just before saying good night, and almost as an afterthought, he asked me whether I liked movies. "Sure, I love movies in German. But then, I might love movies in any language with the right person," I replied.

It was not Dick's looks that attracted me to him. In fact, I could hardly understand what it was—perhaps his open, positive attitude or his firm but friendly way. Or maybe it was his exuberance and unquenchable enthusiasm for life. And soon I discovered his strength of vision and sense of purpose. That's when I decided to marry him. I knew in my heart that the courtship dance that began on Veteran's Day 1961 would blossom and last for the rest of my life. Yet, love is fragile and vulnerable and ends just as unexpectedly as it begins. It could have ended right there in Oxford, and many other times since; but instead we lasted almost thirty-three years as spouses and continue as partners in parenting and grandparenting. The challenge for us now is to transform our chaotic marriage and divorce into a trustworthy friendship.

After that first encounter, I next heard from Dick through a short note. The note seemed discourteous and wasn't at all romantic. "Dagmar," it said—not "Dear Dagmar" or "Dagmar dear." Nothing. Just "Dagmar, I will pick you up for a movie tonight. 6:00 P.M.—OK?" It was initialed, not even signed. I thought, this man may have brains and heart, but he has absolutely no class. Now, after three decades in the United States, that note seems less presumptuous than it appeared to my Austrian self then. But at the time I was offended. What does he mean—he *will* pick me up? How about asking if I would like to be picked up? Yes, we had vaguely discussed the possibility of going out the following evening, but nothing had been decided—so now I am supposed to be ready promptly at 6:00 P.M.? I can't remember exactly what I wrote, but I jotted my reply on his own flimsy note. He picked up on my disgust, came over to my place in person, and of course managed to persuade me to come along to the movie that night.

What continues to please me about this incident is that for the first time in my life I was ready to let go of a relationship because I felt I had been treated disrespectfully. I wish I had strengthened and honed this sense of self and continued to insist on being treated respectfully. Dick never did understand how significant this tiny incident was to me; to him the whole thing was just a linguistic misunderstanding. He did not intend to hurt me; he was just himself, direct and pragmatic. But during the thirty-three years of our marriage, I came to accept and excuse much discourtesy and chose to rationalize even outright betrayals.

Our next date was tea in Dick's room. In Oxford, "tea" was a euphemism for sex, or at the very least messing around. Of course, when I arrived at Oxford, I had not the vaguest notion about that. The first time a British student invited me to his room for tea and then tried to kiss me, I was shocked and enraged and decided then and there to stay away from English men. But I decided to take my chances with this American. We did kiss that afternoon and spent a lovely time with Joan Baez's *Pleasures of Love* playing in the background. We saw each other daily after that.

As Easter break approached, we decided to drive to Paris together. Dick and his friends Ian and Jack McNees had been planning the trip for months. Since I had to get home to Vienna some way and had never been to Paris, I eagerly accepted their offer to take me along. Little did I know that Dick had an American woman friend in Paris and that he was still hoping to become more involved with her. But I never viewed Andrea Cousins as much of a threat. I had fallen in love with Dick and sensed that his feelings for me were growing stronger while his attraction to Andrea was weakening.

After arriving in Paris, Ian, Jack, Dick, and I set out in search of a hotel in the neighborhood of Notre Dame. We had very little money and finally wound up at a sleazy little place that was frequented by transvestites. I clearly remember the man who checked us in; he wore a blonde wig and was dressed up in a glitzy evening gown. He took an immediate liking to Ian and seemed very disappointed when he discovered that the four of us were planning to share a room.

I said yes to sleeping in the same room with these three men. I said yes to sleeping in the same bed with Dick. But I said no to making love before the time was right for me. At that time in my life, I had a very elaborate vision about what my first lovemaking experience would be like. I had to have a deep sense of security and trust. I had to be open to the wildest and most passionate consequences of that moment. If a child would come of such an encounter, I wanted to be able to welcome it joyfully and cherish the blessing of our creative love. I would settle for nothing less than the fullest consummation of physical passion and spiritual creativity.

When we left Paris, we headed on to Zurich, and there I left Ian and Dick and took a train home to Vienna. Dick and I planned to meet the week after Easter in Florence, and we spent a marvelous time together exploring the city and each other. Dick told me at length about his Methodist faith and his opposition to capital punishment and all forms of state-sanctioned violence. I shared with him my belief in the sacredness of marriage and raising children within a Catholic community. On our drive back, somewhere before we crossed over to England, Dick proposed.

My decision to marry Dick was simple and felt natural, almost inevitable. He seemed to have character, brains, and the fortitude to face any and all challenges, and I trusted him to be a good husband and father. I loved this young American's sense of fun and adventure. At his side, my curiosity was aroused and my cravings satisfied. I believed that he would protect me from my worst self. His friendly, caring manner began to heal my many real and imagined childhood wounds, and a whole new woman emerged in his arms. His love was ardent and caring, his respect something I thought I could count on.

I chose Dürnstein for our wedding. Situated along the banks of the Danube, this tiny city was a beautiful and unusually romantic setting. According to legend, King Richard the Lionhearted was captured in a tavern near Vienna one night in December 1192. Attempting to flee his enemies disguised as a pilgrim, he was recognized by his ring, which he had forgotten to remove. He was dragged to the dungeon in Dürnstein's fortress. Legend tells that Richard's faithful servant Blondel went from castle to castle all along the Danube, traveling as a troubadour and singing the king's favorite songs. While singing outside the castle walls at Dürnstein, Blondel heard a voice call out from the depth of the dungeon. And so master and servant found each other and managed to escape together. Some believe that Blondel, which translates as "the one with golden hair," was a woman disguised as a boy; others go so far as to claim the young boy was the king's lover. Certainly, s/he loved the king passionately enough to risk his/her life to rescue him. Whatever version one wishes to believe, Dürnstein is still a perfect place for lovers. I imagined that our wedding ritual, performed in such a setting, steeped in the aura of that other Richard of long ago, would make the ceremony very special.

On August 24, 1962, Dick and I stood before a golden, globe-shaped tabernacle and offered each other the sacrament of holy matrimony. Mutti had sewn my wedding gown. It was very simple and beautiful. Made of a heavy white moiré silk, the long tunic was loosely held together at the waist by a wide pleated cummerbund. Over my dark hair a long white veil hung, graced by the traditional fresh myrtle wreath. I carried a bouquet of red roses.

My best friend at Neuland, Ulli, was the official photographer. (Being the creative type, her pictures turned out a bit blurred, but very artistic.) Dieter Sauermann was my "best man," and Michael Smyth, from Australia, was Dick's. Dick's father, Frank, who was then mayor of Lakewood, Ohio, sent the mayor of Dürnstein a special greeting with a request to extend every possible courtesy to his son. The mayor of Dürnstein, the smallest city in Europe, was very pleased, and we received special treatment indeed.

Throughout the civil ceremony that preceded the church wedding, both Dick and I were extremely nervous. The movie of our wedding shows me wide eyed and records Dick's repeated gulping. Many years later, when we showed this film to our highly amused teenagers, I think it was Natalie who blurted out in complete astonishment, "My God, Dagi, you were so young, and Dick looks so skinny. How did you know that this lanky lad would one day become such a good-looking guy?" I thought of him as handsome and sexy then and have never changed my mind about that. But to my daughters, that was the best example of blind love they had ever seen. They concluded that I was just lucky that he had turned out so well. The kids also wanted to know whether I suspected Dick had political ambitions way back then. I told them that in 1962 he claimed that his dream was to become a high school teacher and eventually a principal.

Twenty-five years later, we returned to Dürnstein and stood before the same altar to renew our vows. This time, the promises were made in English. I thought it wonderfully appropriate that the tabernacle was in the shape of the globe, for together we had circled it many times and perhaps even helped change a small part of it for the better. I wondered then whether we would continue to have enough gratitude and fortitude to stay the course, consecrated to each other, and win this race of a lifetime. Sometimes our cultural and denominational differences seemed to get the better of us, and at these times we clung to each other simply to beat the odds. From the start, our families presented difficulties.

The adventure and romance I experienced in our marriage surpasses any feeling of wonder and delight I have ever felt elsewhere before, during, or since our time together. Maybe it was the fact that we could not understand each other's language well and had to learn to communicate in ways beyond words. Maybe it was because we chose to accept our own and each other's vulnerabilities with humility

71

and awe and learned to celebrate the mystery we shared. Together we raised six children and were present for the births of most of our grandchildren. Together we survived public life and public scrutiny. For more than three decades we empowered each other to grow, change, and do so much more together than either of us could have dreamed or hoped to do alone. From the very beginning, we had this naive notion that together we were better, and we knew deep down that apart was not part of the plan. We trusted that a power greater than ourselves had brought us together and would continue to keep us united in our partnership. When our song asked, "Do you believe we can do together all the things we can't do alone?" we answered, "Yes! We do."

But there is much I learned to do alone in our sometimes troubled and often surprisingly joyful years together. I learned to speak and write English. I got my first driver's license in India, where I had to learn to accommodate chaos and the unexpected—appropriate training for the personal and political challenges to come. I learned to stand by my convictions and speak in public. I learned to trust and love myself and other women. I learned to endure the pain of betrayal and the continuous frustration with distortions and misrepresentations of plans and aspirations. I developed a thicker skin and a better sense of humor. I learned to be grateful for an amazing partnership with a husband who had the heart of a lion. And I learned that in life and love, nothing is certain except that everything will change.

6

"I want it to be all that it can be"

we are a mystery which will
never happen again
a miracle which has never happened before
—*E.E. Cummings*

Columbus, Ohio
Halloween and All Saints Day, 1995
This evening I saw coverage on the evening news of a simple, peaceful pagan ceremony in respectful remembrance of the many pagans who died during the Burning Times in Europe. Unfortunately, that piece was followed by a report that some criminal cultists—or perhaps just some angry, confused young people—marked this Halloween night by torturing and killing black cats because they believed them to be demons of darkness. The way in which the news reports were constructed left me with the feeling that both groups were bad news. But I know better: those who love and respect Mother Nature and all her creatures, even down to the feline familiars, and those who exploit and destroy her diverse species are in no way comparable.

I am delighted that our oldest grandchild, Eleanor, dressed up as a black cat for Halloween this year. Max, her brother, was a knight in shining armor brandishing, with equal exuberance, a plastic Excalibur and a bright-orange pumpkin bucket. He seemed more dangerous to me than his older sister or even his younger sister, Julia, who trick-or-treated as the Wild Thing from the wonderful book Where the Wild Things Are.

Perhaps the most positive aspect of the Halloween tradition is that it encourages us to accept the polarity of darkness and light and affirm the possibility of facing and overcoming our own shadow side. Then, just as candy is the reward for venturing into the dark tonight, so too do swift, predictably sweet rewards await those willing to brave the daunting tasks of accepting all we are and becoming all we are meant to be.

In Austria we do not celebrate Halloween. Instead, the Devil (Krampus) gets his due on December 6, the feast of Saint Nicholas, when adults disguised as bishops and devils roam the streets and surprise anxious children in their very homes. They reward the children for being good and punish them for being bad; but since no one is all bad or good all the time, everyone receives sweets and nuts from the saintly Nicholas, and even the best little boys and girls get whacked by Krampus's switch. Unfortunately, in our home only Krampus ever showed up. As an adult, I can see the truth and the humor in such a tradition, but as a little girl I was terror stricken by the sight of my father in his Krampus disguise. No matter how many goodies Saint Nicholas left in my boots, they never made up for the fear and humiliation experienced by this often public exposure of my hidden flaws. (I am now aware that the historic Saint Nicholas never had the demon in tow; he simply saved the life of a dark-skinned man who, from that day on, never left his side and faithfully served him until death. How entrenched the racism of those good folks in the pews must have been to transform a good, faithful servant into a frightening devil!)

For one night a year, Halloween lets us pretend to be anything or anyone we wish. By illuminating and decorating our homes with fanciful hand-carved pumpkins and in receiving strangers with sweet hospitality, we welcome the darkness of winter without losing faith in future springs. Any feast that brings light into darkness has a healing effect, helping us to remember that by welcoming what we fear, we overcome the biggest fear of all—the fear of death.

All Souls Day is a more somber, silent feast in which we remember those we loved who have passed on. After the spooky, rowdy night of goblins, monsters, dragons, and demons, a fresh morning of peace breaks. Death is inevitable, mysterious, and frightening, but it will not have the last word, ever. Whether we believe in the Christian Good News or not, all of us share the hope that one day we will be reunited with all in love and light. Call it what you will—energy returning to the source; springtime, when seeds planted deep in the soil awake and start to reach toward the sun; a return home to our ancestors; a spiritual wedding or union with the beloved; cocoons broken open by winged dancing. To our amazement, we come to realize that the darker the night of the soul the more visible even the smallest spark of hope. In their book Trances People Live, *Stephen Wolinsky and Margaret O. Ryan write, "There is a profound difference between focusing our energy on battling evil (like addictions) versus focusing our energy on seeking our own goodness and spirituality. If change cannot be effected through the conscious mind, then the therapist turns to the unconscious for resources. If still none is forthcoming, the therapist can move on further into the collective unconscious in search of resources that will shift the subjective experience from problem states to stages of recovering."[1] Feasts and rituals do just that: choosing to join the celebration of any collective tradition is always an invitation to become willing to shift our consciousness, which in turn helps us to grow together in community.*

Unfortunately, too many of our fairy tales continue to depend on goblins and witches to embody our own shadows. In one of my favorite fairy tales, "Hansel and Gretel," the old witch is stuffed in the oven by the little girl to save her big brother. Gretel's burnt offering of the old lady is the sacrifice necessary to help them survive, and Hansel's leadership is essential to the pair finding their way out of the murderous forest. You'll remember that the only woman more fearsome and dangerous to the children than the witch is the stepmother, who robs the children of their father's affections. The irony in the Grimm Brothers' version of the story is that the father is impotent—off the hook, so to speak—and the real mother is dead.

Rarely is the witch a man. In the Middle Ages, clerics were encouraged to hunt down women suspected of practicing witchcraft and the Church sanctioned torturing them in the most perverse and obscene fashion. If a confession could not be extracted, these women were executed—burned at the stake for the sake of their immortal souls. To this day, women still share in the collective trauma of those millions who were hunted down and murdered for nothing more than being autonomous, often older, healers, herbalists, and midwives—the original scientists of the human race. Daughters were made to watch their mothers' executions so as to sear into them

---

1. Stephen Wolinsky, with Margaret O. Ryan, *Trances People Live: Healing Approaches in Quantum Psychology* (Bramble, 1992).

the fear of being a female and impress on them the danger inherent in iden-
tifying with women. Those millions of women burned at the stake impressed
on our collective subconscious the idea that women cannot depend on other
women for their survival, that without the patriarchal protection of father,
husband, son, priest, soldier, or other sovereign, we have no rights—to love
or even live. Is this why so many of us choose to bury feelings we have for
each other, why love for and among women continues to be minimized,
trivialized, and undermined?

    In Odd Girls and Twilight Lovers, *Lillian Faderman recounts the*
history of lesbian life over the past one hundred years. What she shows con-
vincingly and gracefully is that "not only are lesbians as diverse as the fe-
male heterosexual population, but if any generalization can be made about
large numbers of them at any given time, it is bound to change anyway.
The only constant truth about The Lesbian in America has been that she
prefers women. In that sense, those of us who prefer men cannot consider
ourselves to be lesbian any more than those who prefer women can call
themselves heterosexual."² But where does that leave those of us who pre-
fer not to limit our choices by gender, race, religion, or nationality?

    And while I certainly do not believe that any of us are helpless genetic
entities incapable of determining the direction and depth of our erotic
affections and encounters, I have come to understand that sexual addictions
exist and that they are progressive and potentially lethal to body, mind, and
soul. Up to a certain point, we might have had the power or desire to choose
right from wrong, healthy from unhealthy, or constructive from destruc-
tive behavior; but as the compulsion progresses, we often capitulate and lose
our very soul to it. Only then, when we freely choose to acknowledge our
own powerlessness, can we recover. So to encourage, or force, people to tell
less than the truth about who they are and who they love is to become part
of the problem.

    The dilemma for me was not whether the public had the right to know
about our personal lives, but whether we had the right to keep some of our

2. Lillian Faderman, *Odd Girls and Twilight Lovers: A History of Lesbian Life in Twen-*
tieth-Century America (Penguin, 1992).

personal loves private. The question was whether the feminist mantra "the personal is political" excluded the sexual. Dick and I agreed to keep our sexual needs and experiences private. Today I am less sure where, when, and how to draw that line and whether refusing to lie is honest enough. "I try to be transparent in my human relations and in my work. But, of course, that makes you very vulnerable and very few people dare. It's too dangerous."³ But to strive for less than that much is no safer.

I n retrospect, it seems incredible how quickly our love ignited. We met in November 1961, were married the following August, and arrived in New Haven that September, just in time for Dick to begin work on a master's degree in education at Yale University. Life was moving at breakneck speed. Less than a year after meeting Dick, I was a married woman, a naturalized alien, an expectant mother—and very happy.

In New Haven, I had to adjust to a new life-style, language, and culture. We had no money to speak of, and simple tasks posed real challenges. Grocery shopping, for instance, tested my language skills, and patience. I had great difficulty reading the labels and recognizing ingredients and food items; nothing was what it seemed; the content of the boxes bore no resemblance to the pictures on the labels. Our tenement flat also presented problems. The stove was temperamental and worked only sporadically, so to keep the oven door from popping open while baking, we had to wedge rags in the door, which meant that dinner could have burst into flames at any moment.

Growing up in Austria, I missed noticing that America had its share of poor people. If there is one overriding myth all over the world about the United States, it is that all Americans are rich, drive enormous cars, and have TVs in every room and a swimming pool in every backyard. Imagine my bewilderment when I discovered that my first home

3. May Sarton, *At Seventy: A Journal* (W. W. Norton, 1984).

in America had no TV, no swimming pool, no yard—not even grass around the building—and that the electrical appliances were downright dangerous to operate. Wedding gift money paid for the weekly excursion to the food co-op, and had it not been for the generosity of our fathers, we might not have survived those first couple of winter months at the edge of Dick's grand alma mater in the heart of New Haven's Oak Street slum.

Fortunately, I did manage to find a job—which seems incredible to me today. Though I barely spoke English, I convinced someone at the Yale Main Library to hire me. After all, I reasoned confidently, I spoke two other languages fluently, and my English was bound to improve. I was hired into the catalog department, where I translated cards from German and Italian to English and filed them in the appropriate place. I earned just enough to pay the rent and Dick made up the difference with his part-time job. But groceries and electricity, water, and telephone bills, not to mention books, were financial challenges that seemed to overwhelm us right from the start, and throughout our marriage the lack of money never stopped being a problem.

Except for our time in India, from 1963 to 1967, and the eight years in the Governor's Residence, we seemed to always end up robbing Peter to pay Paul. Raising six children in America between 1962 and 1992 was anything but easy. I will always remember Dick sitting at the kitchen table valiantly trying to make ends meet. My family helped by sending money every Christmas and giving us the down payments for our homes, and Dick's father continued to pour financial resources into our political campaigns. But I still do not remember a day when we were not worried about money.

Maybe those continuous financial worries helped me develop a sincere empathy for anyone trying to raise one child, let alone more, without the help of a partner. No doubt my own experience has taught me that parenting can be great fun, but it also means worries and hard work. And raising children in America is very costly. Physically, emotionally, and spiritually, child-rearing is backbreaking, exhausting labor that goes financially unrewarded in our economy. Those of us who spend our most productive years raising the next generation of Social Security payers do not qualify for any old-age financial security ourselves, nor do we have continued access to our children's fathers' future earnings and pensions once they decide to leave.

I did have a taste of this discrimination early on, when—as I was growing bigger by the day and finding it harder and harder to fit in between the stacks—we discovered that the fine print of my health policy at the library excluded pregnancy benefits for the first nine months of employment. Of course, Dick was fully covered—no nine-month exclusion for him. Since health insurance was essential for my condition, Dick began to look for a better-paying job with better benefits. He had been teaching part time in an inner-city public school, struggling with the challenges posed by racism and poverty and becoming disillusioned with the master's program. At the time, Yale saw itself training teachers primarily for private schools, and he had no interest in a teaching career in private schools. It was around then that his interest in teaching as a way to change lives began to give way to his interest in using politics as a way to change education.

One of our early informative political connections came, oddly enough, by way of the laundromat. Once a week I'd take our wash to the local laundromat, which unbeknownst to me was a favorite hangout for the Oak Street gang. I had never heard of gangs and did not realize how deep-seated their hatred was for Yalies. Bobbie Grayson, the gang's leader, was a young, angry black man who was paralyzed from the waist down. Despite his considerable handicap, he was feared and respected by his peers. He later told us that he came to be their leader because he was the fastest with knives: "All I have to do is make sure that my back is covered, preferably against some wall, and then nobody can touch me." Like family, his gang members cared for all his personal needs and took him wherever they went. They seemed nice company to me, and during my weekly visits we talked about books, movies, family, travel, and sports.

Then one day Dick came along. As soon as he entered the laundromat, the whole atmosphere changed. It was clear that he was not welcome, especially when they discovered that he was a student at Yale. After some heated whispered consultations with his gang, Bobbie turned to me and simply said, "He's lucky he's with you, and you're lucky we did not know you were married to a Yalie."

We were even luckier to have met Bobbie. It wasn't long before his friends were bringing him up to our place about once a week, and he was sharing his hopes and dreams with us. He wanted a place of his own, a youth center for his neighborhood, and respect for his race. When he discovered that I was pregnant, he was awed and elated and turned to Dick and said, "A child, Dick, is a great responsibility. To be a good father ain't easy. But, remember, loving their mom is free and is the best you'll ever do for your kids." My friendship with Bobbie Grayson taught me much about the incredible chasms between black and white and rich and poor in America.

Early on Dick and I forged some important, lasting friendships. My best friend in New Haven was Miette Alpert, a French woman married to a Connecticut newspaper reporter. Miette was another charmed soul (or so I thought) who, just like my friend Doris in Vienna, seemed to have everything—an adoring husband, a well-established place in society, good taste, comfortable income, antiques and oriental carpets, books and music, and my all-time favorite car, a Jaguar. But after her first husband died, Miette was not so lucky with her second marriage. She was probably the first battered woman I knew. Bill Coffin, the chaplain at Yale, and his wife, Eva Rubinstein were another young couple we spent time with. I admired them, for they already had the family I yearned to have, and was entranced by how much warmth and passion they seemed to exude. When, years later, their marriage split apart, I was deeply saddened and felt the first traces of fear for my own union.

· · ·

Despite the many hardships, our life seemed charmed. Notwithstanding our lack of money, we managed to have a good time with our friends and frequently had them over for dinner. I knew how to make meals out of nothing and received much positive feedback for my budding culinary skills. (By American standards, I was a good cook; in Austria I would have barely passed muster.)

We planned to spend our first Christmas as a married couple with Dick's family. Since we had no money for gifts, I decided to bake cookies instead. I bought a twenty-five-pound bag of flour and a ten-pound bag of sugar and scrimped on meat in our daily meals so I could invest in butter, nuts, and chocolate. I then started baking—every day a different recipe. By the end of Advent, I had filled an enormous canister with all kinds of wonderful cookies. They smelled, looked, and tasted grand. The praise I received and the pleasure those cookies brought to the whole Celeste family was well worth the many weeks of scrimping on food and baking into the early morning hours. To this day, baking and doing special things for my family at Christmas has remained one of my favorite rituals.

Some of the most extraordinary times at the Governor's Residence were the many fabulous Christmas seasons we were privileged to celebrate there. The holiday season always began with Advent caroling evenings, an Austrian tradition I carried on in my own family. Advent has always been my favorite of all family celebrations. Every Sunday in Advent, Dick, the children, and I would gather around the Advent wreath, sing Christmas carols, and read Scripture accounts and other Christmas stories. We'd sample that week's batch of Christmas cookies and usually end the evening with more singing. The Advent tradition grew after Dick became governor, when on Joy Sunday (the third Sunday in Advent) the celebration at the Residence included the Columbus Newman Center choir. Dick extended the welcome and read from the Scripture, the choir led the singing, and Father Sam Ciccolini, from the Interval Brotherhood in Akron, gave the blessing. Guests brought homemade cookies to share, and children were always welcome. After a private, family Christmas Eve and Christmas Day in the Governor's Residence, the public celebrations continued with an all-day open house featuring refreshments and costumed singers from the Ohio Historical Society on the Feast of St. Stephen. (But during our years in office, Christmas really began much earlier in the year, when Bobbie Wiard, the Residence manager, and I began to search for an Ohio craftsperson to design a small official gift, at an affordable price, to be shared with cabinet and staff members and friends across the country and around the world. We also worked months in advance on the governor's Christmas card, always searching for a complementary greeting to grace the still-life drawings of the festively decorated Residence done by Ohio artist Robert Laessig.)

The heart of the season for the Celeste family was Christmas Eve. From our own first Christmas in India to our last one in 1994 at our home in Victorian Village in Columbus, the best time for me was that moment when the door finally opened and we caught the first glimpse of the candles flickering on the biggest possible fresh-cut tree, covered with ornaments and home-baked edibles. To see those tiny flames reflected brightly in the eyes of the smallest ones in our family was Christmas at its best. I hope I will continue to enjoy that real Christmas spirit with our children and theirs for many years to come.

When we returned to New Haven after celebrating Christmas, Dick received an invitation to go to Washington and meet with Sally Bowles and others who were busy designing the latest agency addition to the Kennedy administration, the Peace Corps. Dick had grown impatient with Yale and was eager for a change. He accepted the appointment to become a Peace Corps liaison officer for Latin America. Arguably the truest expression of the New Frontier spirit, the Peace Corps was a truly exciting enterprise, and it was an honor and a privilege to be part of it. He was happy to be a part of Camelot, and I was happy at home waiting for our first baby.

As undersecretary of state, Chester Bowles, Sally's father, had been one of the voices in opposition to the Cuban invasion and the buildup in Vietnam. He thereafter became persona non grata, especially to some of the more hawkish advisers in President Kennedy's inner circle. Dean Rusk was chosen over Chet as secretary of state, probably because he could be trusted to let the president act as his own secretary of state. Then, after the failure of the Cuban invasion, those who should have taken the blame projected it onto those, like Bowles, who had tried to warn the president. Rusk and others wanted Bowles off the seventh floor of the State Department, but President Kennedy appreciated Chet's integrity and intelligence and wanted to keep him close. All Bowles was willing to accept, instead of secretary of state, was another tour as ambassador to India. That turn of events became a most welcome opportunity and adventure for us.

Dick had met Steb Bowles, Chet's second wife, at a congressional hearing in 1959. He had gone to Washington to testify against the draft. Steb watched the proceedings, and after the hearing introduced herself to Dick and shared with him her surprise that, as a Yale man, he had that point of view. She told him that her son Sam was at Yale, too, and encouraged them to get together. And so they did. Together, Dick and Sam organized one of the most extraordinary events spawned by that supposedly "silent generation." Dick had won a $2,000 award, the Hatch Peace Prize, and decided to invest the money into Challenge, an organization he and Sam and others had created to raise awareness about the dangers of the nuclear age. They organized a concert that would bring Odetta, Pete Seeger, and many other musicians to Yale. Along with the music event, they also offered seminars on "The Challenge of Surviving in the Nuclear Age." That event was a forerunner of what later became known as "teach-ins, " which were designed primarily to put an end to the war in Vietnam but also to put to rest the notion that war in the nuclear age was still a viable option.

That chance meeting with Steb Bowles and the work with Sam on Challenge opened the door for Dick and me to one of the most extraordinary experiences of our life—a four-year diplomatic tour in India. It also initiated a lifelong friendship with many in the Bowles' circle. Chet and Steb taught us that familial commitments can extend beyond blood relatives and that a political constituency is at heart an extension of such a circle of friends. They were classic liberals. They saw crisis as opportunity, realistically assessed problems, and courageously developed personal and political solutions. They had the will and usually the resources to take that essential next step; they did something about the problems they saw and moved to solve them with utmost civility, conviction, and deep compassion. Steb especially represented to me the epitome of tolerance and goodwill. As a trained social worker and psychiatric nurse, her natural response to outcasts and oppressed people was empathy. I feel privileged to have known Chet and Steb and loved them both very much.

Whenever Dick was traveling to the various Peace Corps training camps, I would move into the Bowles' residence in Georgetown so I could feel safe. Our own apartment in the basement of a Capitol Hill townhouse was anything but safe. A few weeks after we moved in, a woman was killed on her way out of the neighborhood Catholic church, and often we were awakened in the middle of the night by gunshots nearby. But the rats terrified me almost more than the random violence. No matter how many we poisoned or trapped, there were always more to take their place.

Life with Chet and Steb in Georgetown was very different from that of struggling newlyweds. Every evening interesting people would join us for dinner, or Chet and Steb would take me along to parties. I vividly remember the time we went for brunch at Drew Pearson's farm. The guests were an impressive selection of Washington's insiders . . . and me. I was not only a nobody, but I did not even have enough sense to know it. I so completely lacked experience with America's elite and Washington society that I never even felt out of place. Despite the fact that I was very young, and very pregnant, jaded journalists and earnest political types seemed to enjoy my company. I suppose I cared more about ideas than issues and was bold and passionate and innocent enough to freely speak my mind.

At the Pearson brunch table, I found myself seated next to a very interesting and refreshingly outspoken older gentleman. We got into quite a heated discussion about the merits of common law versus Roman law and the need to develop an international system including the best of both in order to begin the arduous task of settling global disputes peacefully through the world courts. The rest of the table had stopped talking when I told my amused partner that I just could not agree with him on some legal point or other. When Dick returned from his trip, I told him what fun I'd had at the farm and how my conversation with my dinner partner seemed to have been the center of attention.

"What did you say his name was?" he asked.

"Oh, you know I can't remember names," I replied. "Something like Chief Judge Warner or something."

Alarmed, he asked, "Chief Justice Earl Warren? You argued points of international law with the Chief Justice?"

"Well, he was very nice, and I did even manage to persuade him of a point or two," I said, very pleased with myself.

"Oh, my God" was all my stunned spouse could say.

The next day Dick called Chet at the State Department to apologize for my outspokenness, only to hear Chet laugh out loud and say, "Dick, forget it. She was marvelous. Just twenty-one years old and so bright and well informed—she and Earl were the best thing going there." From then on, throughout the many years with Chet and Steb, I was always "just twenty-one" and a delight to them because I dared to be open, outspoken, and completely myself. It was only after meeting them that I began to realize that I was bright and brave and better prepared than most for a life in politics.

One morning at Kovolum in Kerala, just after we'd arrived in India, Chet and I were floating together on one of those simple but extremely efficient Indian log boats. Although this boat was just a hollowed-out log it somehow could not only hold its own against the waves but could comfortably accommodate two adults. It was a perfect morning, the water calm, the sun not too hot. The colors of the sky and water were almost identical, a mixture of emerald green and sapphire blue. It was out of the blue that Chet turned to me and asked, "Do you think you are ready for the rough-and-tumble of American politics?" I told him that I'd not yet voted in an American election but wondered why I had to worry about politics. He then gently but firmly said, "Dick will be involved politically soon; he will be very good at it—mark my words. And you will either love it or hate it. If you love it, you'll have a ball and do much good; if you hate it, Dick will have a much harder time, and neither of you will be able to do all the good you can do together." He shared with me his hopes for Dick and his dream that someone from the many young people he trained throughout his own public life would continue what he had set out to do.

He also promised that his contribution to the effort would be to take us on a two-month vacation every year. "No job is worth it unless you can take off at least two months a year," he told me. We took only one of those vacations, sailing *Nordlys,* a seventy-eight-foot sailboat designed by Chet. He was a good politician, and a better diplomat, but he was at his best at the helm of a sailboat. On our sailing trip, Chet spent much time telling stories about the past, analyzing the present, and projecting positive hopes for the future. In fact, he was the most hopeful person I've ever known. Dick and I relished our time with him.

Steb (formerly Dorothy Stebbins) was also a role model for me but in quite a different way. While Chet thought out loud and gave clear instructions, Steb was more indirect. She could make you laugh with her irreverent language and ideas but was essentially a very private person. As time went on, she became even more quiet and withdrawn. Very open-minded (possibly because of her own experience with depression and manic episodes following some brain surgery early in her youth), Steb accepted people from all walks of life and felt deep empathy for those who were caught in webs of confusion and pain. She and Chet managed to raise their own three children and kept an open home and heart for the children from Chet's first marriage. Before meeting them, I had never encountered people who had to face the challenge of blending families after divorce. At the time it all seemed very natural, but today I realize how exceptional they were.

Their public life was productive and successful. Chet accumulated his wealth during his first marriage and was a millionaire before he turned thirty. Benton & Bowles rapidly became one of the most successful advertising companies in America. The money he had certainly helped pave his public path, but it was still a sometimes rocky one, filled with many ups and downs and twists and turns. Steb was most disappointed by his defeat for reelection as governor of Connecticut in 1950 and never forgave those inside and outside the party who deserted and betrayed him.

Chet's first tour as American ambassador to India was probably the greatest growing experience for both of them. By the time Dick and I had a chance to return to India with them in 1963, with Dick acting as Chet's executive assistant, Steb was an experienced hand at meeting the challenges and criticisms they both faced. She loved the country deeply, immersing herself in Indian music and art, and brought Indians from all walks of life to Roosevelt House, the official residence of the American ambassador in New Delhi. Chet asked for my help in improving the menu plans. Together with Bim Bissell, the ambassador's social secretary, we planned some of the most spectacular events for both the American and Indian communities: Diwali parties, complete with thousands of oil lamps decorating the residence; musical events in candlelit ancient ruins; picnics and dinners and cocktail parties at Ratendon Road (Chet and Steb's real, unofficial home); the lavish Fourth of July open houses at Roosevelt House; and the annual Christmas open houses, which attracted thousands of guests. (I was in charge of decorating the tree and was amazed to discover that the baked goods and popcorn strings attracted hundreds of tropical birds who came flying through the open doors from the residence gardens. It was the most lively and enchanting Christmas tree I'd ever seen!) A great advocate of contemporary American artists, Steb filled Roosevelt House with a spectacular collection of twentieth-century American art and welcomed American artists and musicians visiting India. One of my most vivid memories is of Duke Ellington playing for us long into the night.

Much of what I later brought to the role of First Lady of Ohio I learned from Steb. By example, she taught me that I could be a good public partner without losing my identity or sense of humor. She was an iconoclast, and so was I. She did not believe in formality, doing away with mandatory hats and gloves for women at embassy receptions and challenging the tradition of dropping calling cards. When she grew bored with the stuffiness of diplomacy, she often made waves by making people laugh. One day I accompanied Steb to a synchronized swimming event at the American Embassy Club, staged by the wives of the foreign service officers in New Delhi. The women tried their best, but the show was still pretty awful. During one of the interminable intermissions, Steb turned to me and said, "Hang on to my purse." Before I knew it she was off, only to shortly reappear on the diving board. In full regalia (she usually wore magnificent silk saris), she looked around the crowd, waved, smiled, and then, to everyone's horror, jumped into the pool. The Marine Corps security guards were too stunned to react. When she surfaced, she made a few feeble moves mocking synchronized swimming before climbing out of the pool to loud cheers and applause. She had found a most interesting way of being excused from watching the rest of the show.

Still, there was a shadow side to Steb's life, which she bore with great dignity. The medications she took for her manic depression, and the social expectations of the life she led, eventually took their toll. In her seventies, she faced the harsh reality of her own chemical dependency. I don't think she ever warmed to Alcoholics Anonymous (AA), but I know she lived an honest recovery program for many years. In retrospect, I am probably most grateful for that example. Over the years she had to endure a great deal of gossip and criticism, but I never once heard her express bitterness or even surprise. Sometimes I thought that some of the people closest to her seemed to be the most judgmental, but either she just did not realize that or had learned to ignore it. Her attitude offered up another lesson that would later help me to withstand many an insider's haughty insensitivity. Steb's relationship with Chet was somewhat mysterious to me. By the time we met, there seemed to be no physical passion between them, yet there was clearly a great deal of affection that bound them together. They were each other's greatest fans and loyal partners to the end. At the time I hoped that would be a pattern for my own marriage, for I believed that Dick and I were meant to pick up where Chet and Steb left off. And for many years, we did.

After Chet was diagnosed with Parkinson's disease in 1963, things changed radically. At first the changes were subtle. He talked less and listened more. "May 30th," the decades-old annual get-together of the "Chet Set" at their home in Essex, Connecticut, became less a political happening and more a family affair. Their own children seldom came, but some of the grandchildren were usually there. For us and our kids, the trip from Ohio to Connecticut became a yearly pilgrimage and often the only family vacation we could afford. With more and more kids stuffed into bigger and bigger vehicles, singing every kind of song we could think of and discussing every imaginable subject, we made our way east. When I look back now, we should have listened to Chet's advice. We never allowed for a one-month vacation, let alone two. But with May 30th, Chet continued to finance our family vacations for many years.

By the time Dick and I were invited to the annual gatherings of family and special friends, many in the group had experienced successes and failures together over and over again. There were those who remembered the good old OPA days, when Chet had been appointed by President Roosevelt to head the Office of Price Administration. Some had been part of Chet's winning and losing campaigns for governor of Connecticut and had hoped for a presidential future for him. Others had worked with Chet in India the first time around and had witnessed his struggles as undersecretary of state. Even though we were the youngest addition to the Chet Set, the experienced hands and old-timers never once made us feel out of place. On the contrary, we represented their hope for the future.

In addition to at least three generations of adults, there were all kinds of young people. Almost everyone brought their kids, infants to teens. There were few rules, and children of all sizes and ages were permitted to roam around free as birds with no curfew or bedtime. There was an unlimited supply of soft drinks and a daily visit by the ice cream man to complete this perfect weekend for children of all ages. Throughout all the fun and frolic and food and drink, there was animated conversation. We discussed everyone and everything. We tested new ideas. We agonized over Vietnam and campus upheavals and the plight of blacks, women, and children. And while everyone thought of themselves as liberal, God knows we did not always agree. The old-timers seemed conservative to us newcomers, and those with responsibilities in the various national administrations struck us as downright trapped. But Chet and Steb taught us all that in diversity lies personal and political strength.

Until Parkinson's forced Chet into a world of silence in the late 1960s, he sat in his chair in the living room as group after group gathered around him to partake of his wisdom, common sense, and humor. Steb often sat at the long table on the side porch surrounded by the younger set. In the evening, the groups converged indoors and composed irreverent musical commentaries on the state of the union to be performed by those of us brave enough to put ourselves on display. The weekend concluded with a traditional touch-football game, which eventually came to include those females willing to risk their limbs and lives. To this day, our kids treasure their memories of those good family times.

In the early 1970s, when we were contemplating our first campaign, Dick and I decided to start our own tradition patterned after May 30th. Joyce Sawyer helped me pull together our first Willaloo. For the next twenty years we brought together family and friends at these annual gatherings held the first weekend after Labor Day at one of the many Ohio state parks. The primary purpose of Willaloo was to enjoy each other's company. But, being political, we dedicated the first morning of the weekend to catching up with everyone's various causes and plotting someone's political campaign—more often than not our own. With that working session behind us, the focus then switched to fun—swimming, hiking, tennis, touch-football, and charades and poker in the evening. Saturday night featured a steak roast and potluck, and we ended Willaloo with a pancake breakfast cooked by Dick and organized by Dora Globe, his loyal assistant for many years. Both Willaloo and Memorial Day traditions continue today with the annual Family Fest at Himmelblau House on Kelley's Island.

I am very grateful that Chet lived long enough to see Dick sworn in as lieutenant governor of Ohio. And I am just as grateful that Steb, while widowed and frail, was determined to come to Ohio to participate in the second inaugural as governor in 1986 as well. She told me then that, to her, Dick's reelection was important because it vindicated, in a small way, the fact that Chet had not been able to win his reelection to the governorship. He had tried to change too much, too fast. Maybe if he had been able to hold on to the governorship, he would have been able to go on to the presidency. Dick did follow in Chet's footsteps—but in reverse. He began with the foreign service, became director of the Peace Corps, and then won the governorship. Only after leaving public life a quarter of a century later did he decide seriously to invest his energy into making money. Ironically, his newfound wealth became a greater stumbling block to our family's health than all the financial hardships of the past.

. . .

In 1963 I knew nothing about the future awaiting me. As much as I loved Dick, I did not feel at home in New Haven or Washington or, least of all, Cleveland. New Delhi felt like home. That first year in America offered me many obstacles and barriers, but the biggest hurdle by far was language. I understood almost everything, and I could speak well enough to engage brilliant men like Chief Justice Warren and Chet in conversation, but I could not put my own language's poetic flow and subtle humor into English. When I married Dick, I never thought about what the loss of my native language would mean to me. I had considered loss of country, religion, friends, parents, even music, but never poetry.

I remember sitting down a few times in our basement flat in Washington, the birth of our first child only weeks away, trying to write so as to better understand all the new impressions and my own feelings and thoughts. To be pregnant for the first time and to have to cope with that momentous experience in a language I hardly knew, and without any female friends or relatives for support, was difficult. Dick had begun his lifelong habits of spending day and night at work, so he was little comfort. I read every baby book in print but had no one to discuss my feelings and thoughts with . . . except for that "little prince" growing inside me. I very much wanted our firstborn to be a boy.

Dick attended with me the first natural childbirth classes offered at Washington Memorial Hospital, which at the time was the only hospital in town willing to allow the father to be present in the delivery room, and also went to baby-care classes at the American Red Cross. Thirty years ago, most men were not encouraged to participate in these momentous events. We felt like pioneers, and we were.

And on June 22, 1963, after a fairly long and strenuous labor, I finally held Eric in my arms. I sat up in bed telling him over and over again, in all the languages I knew, how much I loved him and how relieved and happy I was to have given birth to him, healthy and whole. Dick had been there throughout the birth and was as elated as I.

Dick's mom, Peg, arrived the day I returned home from the hospital and stayed with us for a few days. I was grateful for her help but also anxious around her. Her husband's doubts about my worthiness as a wife for his politically ambitious son were out in the open; but now that I had given birth to Frank Celeste's first grandson, he had finally accepted me. I chose to believe that those negative feelings came from his having been discriminated against as a child born in Italy to an illiterate mother. Frank's school experience in America, which included being told that because he was born in Italy he could never aspire to become president, had given rise to his dream that his son, at least, would be able to do so. Dick's mother's feelings were more complex. She did not want to appear critical, but my ways, just like Frank's mother's ways, seemed not only different but inferior. Based on her limited experience with Frank's southern Italian relatives, "European" to her implied less cultured than "American."

Frank learned at an early age that wealth was equated with worthiness in America. Certainly, he saw it as his duty to provide financial security for his wife and children, but he also saw money as the means of attaining the presidency for his firstborn son. In the end it was not lack of money, or the wrong kind of wife, that brought Richard F. Celeste's presidential aspirations to an abrupt standstill. What ultimately undermined Frank's dream was the example he himself had set. Both Dick and I grew up in families where the man of the house felt entitled to betray his wife, and we continued the pattern, and expanded it to give equal rights to the wife. Like my mother and Peg Celeste, I ended up rationalizing away betrayals in order to keep my family intact. I was persuaded that monogamy and monotony were closely related and that Dick and I could do better than that. Maybe if I had insisted on sexual fidelity, our home might have withstood the conflicts and temptations of these confusing times. Then again, maybe nothing that he could have done would have made enough of a difference, and me insisting on fidelity and integrity might have simply resulted in an earlier divorce.

Arthur Braun, Vati, ca. 1942.

Mutti, Dora Braun, with daughters Dagmar (*left*) and Utzi, ca. 1944.

Austrian refugee children on the bus trip through the Alps on their way to Italy, 1947.

With Zia Maria and Quick in Trieste, 1947.

At Venice's Palazzo San Marco, ca. 1949.

With sister Utzi,
ca. 1950.

On a trip into the Dolomites with Zia Maria and her driver, Nicco, ca. 1950.

Confirmation, 1951.

With confirmation
sponsor Anita
Tomaselli, Trieste,
1951.

Utzi and I in our national
costume, Krems, ca. 1951.

Utzi—perhaps playing an
Elvis record, ca. 1956.

Oma, Mutti, and Utzi, July 1957.

My first formal ball, with
date Peter Miculka, 1958.

With Oxford pals, 1961.

Our wedding day,
Dürnstein, Austria,
August 24, 1962.

Our first home, New Delhi, 1963.

Erik bathing in Kashmir, ca. 1965.

My Indian "mother-
in-law," Sita Nanda,
ca. 1967.

Dick and I with Steb and Chet Bowles, 1967.

The Celeste family, Delaware, Ohio, ca. 1977.

Relaxing with Gayle Channing, Delaware, ca. 1977. Gayle served as my chief of staff from 1983 to 1985.

Campaigning in
Akron, 1978.

With Jimmy Carter upon my posting to the Commission on Higher
Education, July 1978.

A tired Noelle and Stephen out on the campaign trail, ca. 1982.

With Coretta Scott King. *Photo by Will Richmond. Courtesy of Baldwin-Wallace College.*

With Mother
Teresa, 1983.

With good friends and family outside the Residence, ca. 1987. Back row
(from left): Roberta Steinbacher, Anda Cook, Peggy Donovan, Shawn
Austin, Steven with my mother, Eric, unknown. Front row: unknown, Dora
Globe, Mary Zone, me, Carol Stringer, Rotrant Moslehner, Mimi Judson.

Upon earning my bachelor's degree from Capital University, 1987.

Dick's chief of staff, Caroline Lukenmeyer (*left*), and my chief of staff, Marlene Longenecker, ca. 1988.

A meeting of the Women's Core Circle at Himmelblau House on Kelley's Island, ca. 1989.

Frank and Peg Celeste on Kelley's Island, ca. 1985.

Dick at a Willaloo at
Mohican State Park,
ca. 1989.

The Celeste family on Kelley's Island, ca. 1987.

Renewal of our vows upon our twenty-fifth wedding anniversary, Dürnstein, Austria, 1987.

Yoruba conferment of chieftancy by Iyalode of Ife, 1988.

At a Habitat building site in Canton, Ohio, 1999. From left: Marvin Robinson, me, Evelyn Hunt, First Lady Hope Taft, and LeeAnn Massucci.

The Nanda sisters and Dick, who was serving as the U.S. ambassador to India, 2000.

Family Fest at Himmelblau House, 2001.

"And I think I can
do something for Ohio"

In the midst of agony and striving
the door suddenly opened.
—*Rabindernath Tagore*

Lakewood, Ohio
November 11, 1995
Last May, my youngest daughter, Natalie, sent me Nessa Rapoport's A
Woman's Book of Grieving. *In her dedication, Natalie tried to express
that same hard and honest internal struggle:*

> *Sometimes it feels that to be woman is to be wronged. To be woman is
> to be abandoned. To be woman is to be silenced. To be woman is to be
> spoken for. To be woman is to suffer. And yet I am so aware that to be
> woman is also . . .*
> *to express*
> *to love*
> *to give*
> *to survive and to create.*

*"But when grief descends," Rapoport writes, "there is no redemption
than in suffering."*

> *Every moment's pain, like a parody of first love afflicts for hours, and
> every day flaunts its eternity. In those days a woman would give all
> she has to get just one thing back. When you meet such a woman, do
> not speak of inner sustenance, of benefit from sorrow or of healing. Do
> not say that time repairs, or talk of moving forward or of growing. Such
> consolations are absurd. Offer only this: I too, have suffered and en-
> dured. In the end, the fiercest love cannot avert the hour of dying. It is*

*the hardest of all learning that the opposite of depression is not happi-
ness, but vitality, to feel alive each minute you are given. Then when
sweetness comes it is most sweet, and when sorrow comes you know its
name. In the aftermath of suffering, you chart each day as an explorer
preceding map or compass, and what you find is—all happiness is
dappled, and even the bleakest tragedy has moments of strange praise.[1]*

Now, in the darkness of this winter of 1995, I am beginning to understand that life is not about happiness or sadness or even suffering: life just
is. I know that now I will have to "become the spouse I wish I'd had" and
marry my muse. The time has come to stop torturing myself and others with
allusions to the good old days or illusions about better times to come. All
that needs to be done right now is for me to hold together the many girls
and women I have been and coax them to come out of hiding. Then, perhaps, one day I will be ready to accept myself with compassion and admit
that no one and no family is immune from sorrow. Maybe then this loneliness will be transformed into welcome solitude.

To someone like myself, who has birthed six children while fully awake
and aware, rebirth is a simple, natural, and comforting metaphor. I know
I can do this. I know how to wait for the right moment in time to begin pushing. I know how to emerge from what seems like an endless transition. I
know how to open wide and surrender. I know that sort of now-or-never
determination when we birth by heart a new paradigm of life and let the
rhythm of our breath become our best guide in moving from one world of
being to another one of becoming.

In Cloudhand and Clenched Fist, *Rhea Y. Miller suggests that "it
is important to understand that a paradigm shift is not a matter of seeing
things more clearly. Rather, it is like perceiving the universe in a different
color. It is not like using a microscope or better eyeglasses or a cleaner window so we can perceive more detail. It is, instead, an entirely different way
of seeing—or knowing. A paradigm shift is a dimensional change."[2]*

1. Nessa Rapoport, *A Woman's Book of Grieving* (Morrow, 1994).
2. Rhea Y. Miller, *Cloudhand, Clenched Fist: Chaos, Crisis, and the Emergence of Community* (LuraMedia, 1996).

Our universe is full of paradoxes. Take, for instance, a vacuum, which we tend to imagine as empty space, void of anything we value. Yet, paradoxically, a vacuum is the very condition most likely to create matter. Stephen Hawking, in A Brief History of Time[3], *tells us that while billions of stars burn in hundreds of thousand of millions of galaxies, the sum total of the energy of the universe is zero. The meaning here is not that the universe is worthless but that energy is never lost unless matter is gained, and matter is never gained unless energy is lost. In a similar vein, those attempting to communicate understand that information is not something added but is that which differentiates. It is at the point we are able to see difference that we come to awareness. Paradoxes defy common sense, and to recognize them is to see the signs of an impending shift of worldview.*

Why, then, when it comes to divorce do I have such tremendous trouble trusting this process of accepting that a "greater truth" will emerge from this pain and chaos? Why is it that even as I begin to trust again, the uncertainty that accompanies the changing paradigm of nuclear families is far from comforting? Perhaps because ideas that force change provoke fear, and having the rug pulled out from under us causes most of us to crash to the floor, angry for a long time. Accepting a paradigm shift is as difficult for most of us as facing an addiction. To succeed, we must acknowledge the problem before we can imagine recovering from it; to survive, we must reimagine ourselves and our habitat. Doing so will take nothing less than trust, courage, discernment, and compassion.

When I was in India in the 1960s, I discovered that the divisions between the rich and poor were even more rigid there than in America and were compounded by the religion-based caste system, which was more impenetrable than class systems based primarily on economics or education. In Europe, class is still structured more along bloodlines than money, and wealth, while valued, is not as revered as

3. Stephen Hawking, *A Brief History of Time: From the Big Bang to Black Holes*, intro. Carl Sagan (Bantam, 1988).

professional, intellectual, or artistic accomplishments. In the United States there is more mobility between groups of people because class and status are mostly based on wealth, and theoretically anyone can aspire to become wealthy. While the political Left indulge in excessive self-bashing and the political Right engage in self-serving victim bashing, folks in the middle simply hope to be lucky and strike it rich. And while "change for change's sake" has become the most widely intoned political mantra, change without conscience is worse than no change at all. Keeping our politics democratic has been far from simple, and most of us do not want to acknowledge that our two parties are becoming one and the same party, representing first and foremost the 5 percent that control more than half of all the wealth.

When Dick first entered the political fray, he talked about wanting to create a "constituency for change with conscience." Most of us believed then that our system, while not perfect, was good enough and that if the rest of the world would only convert to democracy, global harmony would be assured. What we failed to acknowledge then—and what is even more true today—is that the two parties have rigged the rules and made it virtually impossible for interests other than capitalist ones to emerge. While the rest of the world's democracies struggle with parliamentary complexities and diverse systems of representation, our candidates have only to worry about raising as much money as possible and looking good on TV.

In contrast, watching the people of India struggle to meet the challenge of democracy was often inspiring. In the late sixties, outsiders tended to focus on India's weaknesses rather than recognize the valiant efforts of economically and politically restructuring such a vast country and acknowledge that the Indian middle class was expanding and that, at least officially, neutrality was a necessary part of their political strategy.

At this time, feminists the world over are rightly critical about child brides, dowry deaths, widow burning, and, most vicious of all, the destruction of infant girls—all symptoms of deeply entrenched sexism. So I was most surprised at the ordinary Indian's abiding faith in the strength of their women. It was a most complex paradox: women at once devalued and adored. This is embodied in the goddess Kali, who is worshiped in three persons—Virgin, Mother, and Destroyer—and considered the deepest, darkest, and most mysterious spiritual reality in the Hindu parthenon. Just like Mary in the Christian tradition, Kali rules over life and death.

I was introduced to the power of Indian women as soon as I arrived in New Delhi. Dick had already been there a few months to prepare a home for us and get acquainted with his new job. Eric and I had stopped in Vienna to visit my parents. Eric was not yet six weeks old, and was the youngest person ever to receive a diplomatic passport when we started the trip. It seemed unwise to take him all the way to India before his six-week checkup. I also wanted to spend time with Mutti and my other women friends and to process and absorb all I had experienced that first year in America.

By the time we finally joined Dick, he had made friends with the Nanda family's three sisters, Bimla, Padma, and Meena. My first Indian family event was Meena's wedding, a festive Punjabi affair. The music, dancing, food, and rituals were wild and colorful but also strange and ominous. I was disconcerted by the bride not being permitted to participate in many of the premarriage festivities, even though the marriage had not been arranged. Meena and Rajbir knew each other and had dated a bit. In the Nanda family, the women had the right to veto any prospective groom. The very concept of family-arranged marriages felt alien and oppressive to me. Despite what I thought at the time, marriages in India are more long lived than in our culture. The families take responsibility in making sure their young people choose well. Caste, religion, finances, education, temperament, health, looks, and many other criteria come into play in this very ritualized and highly effective spouse-selection process. Best of all, women are almost exclusively in charge and usually place very high value on the compatibility of the families, not just the individuals.

There was a time in my life when I was too quick to judge other cultures' marriage customs. I've since mellowed. When I visited West

Africa on an Ohio trade mission, a group of very well-educated and highly placed women explained to me that monogamy is not all that much better for them than polygamy had been. Before monogamy became law, the first wife always retained her status and respect, and any other spousal addition to the household had to fit into the larger family; a second wife often became good company for the first wife and always was expected to help. "Now," they told me, "our husbands have mistresses who receive all the best while we have all the work of raising the children and running the household." One woman even went so far as to admit that she would prefer being the mistress to being the wife. Contrary to the view that women are the ones who will benefit most from it, monogamy was designed to benefit men. Historically, monogamy made it possible for men to be reasonably sure who their offspring were and also facilitated their control of households by having a claim to whatever property women brought into the marriage. To this day, most women are not given a fair economic share when they choose to divorce, or even when they are divorced against their will. At least in West Africa a man cannot take a second wife unless he can afford to support both. But in the United States one is free to create any number of families and, more often than not, free to abdicate responsibility for their continued financial and emotional support and well-being. Then again, perhaps the proliferation of spouses in America may be a way back to the future by reinventing tribes. New forms of extended family emerge when we are forced to accept step-siblings the age of one's own children and stepmothers the age of one's siblings!

The Indian model of the extended family served us well. Dick, Eric, and I were welcomed warmly into the Nanda family when I decided to participate in Korvachok, a special annual puja (prayer ritual) in which women fast from sunrise to moonrise, either to ensure the health of their husbands or, if they are not married, to improve their chances of finding the right kind of husband. At first I simply was curious about Hindu rituals, especially those practiced only by women. But when I arrived at Bimla's home, I discovered that her mother, Sita Nanda, was taking my participation very seriously. I could participate in the puja only if I adopted her as my mother-in-law; this would mean, then, that Dick would become her only son. Ever after that ceremony, Mama Nanda took pride in Dick's accomplishments as if he truly were one of her own children. Every time he ran for office, she offered special prayers to Kali, and no one believed more in Dick Celeste than my Indian "mother-in-law." When he was up for reelection as governor, Mama Nanda went to Kali's temple and promised to bring her son to do his own proper *pujas* if he won.

Knowing nothing about her vow, in his second term Dick did arrange for a trade mission to India to encourage business partnerships between Ohio and India. A sister-state agreement was signed by Haryana and Ohio, and Dick and I worked very hard to bring Ohio to the attention of the Indian business community and India to the attention of investors at home. While we were visiting, Mama announced that Dick and I had to take her to Kali's temple in Old Delhi so that she could fulfill her vow. The temple was almost deserted that day. We seemed to be the only worshipers, and I felt slightly relieved. I had been told that sometimes live animals were sacrificed to Kali and I was very glad that Mama Nanda had only insisted on special sweets and marigold garlands. For quite a long time she negotiated with the priests in the inner sanctum of the temple. When she finally did return to us, she told us to remove our shoes and then proceeded to paint a third eye on our foreheads. She then handed Dick the box of sweets to present to Kali.

The goddess Kali is the most fearsome of all Indian gods; believed to bring life and death, she feeds on all living things. In her fierce aspect she is a form of Shakti. She is dark, primordial, and very powerful—a naked, untamed energy. Yet for her devotees she is the incomparable protectress, the champion of Sadhama who harnesses and transmutes the instinctive nature into the innate abilities of the soul; she is, above all, the mother of liberation. The Tantric view Kali as the lady of life and her spouse as the lord of death. (At Himmelblau House, I have a small brass image of Kali stomping on her consort—

a humorous "consolation prize" from a friend upon my divorce.) Contrary to the West's idea of Kali as a purely destructive, dark demon, she is worshiped by Indians as the font of every kind of love, which flows into the world only through her agents on earth: women.

Mama Nanda led us out of the temple and back to the taxi. There we found that our Sikh cabdriver—who on the way out had tried to convince us to visit a Sikh holy place instead—had bought us an English version of the Sikh scriptures wrapped beautifully in golden cloth. He gave it to me with a smile and refused reimbursement. We all drove back in silence. I reflected on the interconnection of all gods and the goodness and confluence of all holy people. Mama Nanda was one of those holy people. Her prayers worked wonders, and they continue to bless her extended family. In her simple, loving way, Mama Nanda is the kind of saint I aspire to become.

For as far back as I can remember, I've wanted to be a saint. I must have been in second or third grade when I realized that most of my friends could celebrate their name days because they had been named after "real" saints. (The Catholic Church designates a saint's death day as their feast day, and anyone named after such a saint can claim that feast day as their name day and celebrate it as they would a birthday.) When I asked my mother to tell me a story about Saint Dagmar, she laughed out loud and said, "There's no such person. I guess you'll have to be very good and become your own saint." The idea intrigued me then and still does now. Whenever I mention this to friends or family, I still get the same response I got years ago from my mother—loud laughter. Ulli, my best friend in Vienna, took the joke one step further and had a folk artist friend paint an icon of the future Saint Dagmar, with a peace dove perched on her hand, a long, celestial blue gown, and flowing chestnut hair.

Why is it that most people seem to think that perfection is required for sainthood? My favorite saint story shows how sainthood is less about perfection than perception. Right after Dick's first gubernatorial victory, I needed to take time out, change my pace, and get some well-deserved rest. So Sally Bowles and I decided to travel together to India. I stayed for nearly two months, first with the Nanda-Bissel family and then with Indira Devi at the Hari Krishna Mandi in Poona. Indira Devi was a psychic from childhood and in her twenties was all but overwhelmed by her spiritual experiences, whereupon she sought the guidance of Dilip Kumar Roy, who initiated her into yoga. She soon attained samadhi and began to manifest various yogic powers. In 1953, after a world tour sponsored by the Indian government, these remarkable artists—Indira a dancer and visionary poetess and Dilip a musician and philosopher—wrote the first book for Westerners on the highest experiences of yoga, the spiritual and superphysical phenomena, and on the role of the guru.[4]

I was also determined to see Mother Teresa and ask her to bless me, our family, our state, and especially all the members of Alcoholics Anonymous who were about to celebrate that movement's fiftieth anniversary in Akron, Ohio. I had volunteered at Mother's New Delhi mission in the early 1960s, before she'd become a Nobel Prize–winning celebrity. But in the 1980s, it required some special connections to see her, so "sister" Bim arranged for one of her friends to take me to her.

When we arrived, Mother was busy gathering together the bare essentials to set up a chapel at the leper colony she had recently founded outside of Delhi. A large International Conference on Leprosy was in full swing in New Delhi at that time, and she was busy attending many sessions. No one knew more about the challenge of healing outcasts than this tiny, formidable woman. In her blue-trimmed white sari and plastic thongs, with a large black rosary hanging at her side, her appearance was austere, almost stern. But she was open, warm, and welcoming. Her luminous smile reminded me of sunrises over snow-covered alpine realms. She had a face like weathered cliffs full of deep crevices, and she seemed ancient rather than old.

I asked her to pray for me and Dick and our whole family and all of Ohio. She turned to me and quietly said, "Ohio? What is Ohio?" I explained Ohio was one of the fifty states of the United States, one

4. Dilip Kumar Roy and Indira Devi, *Pilgrims of the Stars* (Macmillan, 1973).

of the larger states right at the heart of all the others. She tensed a bit and then firmly proclaimed that none of her orphaned children were to be sent to the United States any longer. Since many of the volunteers I had met that day were American women, I was a bit perplexed and asked her why, reminding her that there are plenty of good people who want to adopt in the United States. "Too many divorces, too many abortions, not a good place to raise children, not enough love, too materialistic!" were the reasons she rattled off. Part of me could see Mother Teresa's point and even empathize with her view. Still, I tried to express to her that many of us do the best we can as parents and that things are not as bad as they seem to be on television. She remained unconvinced, I am sure.

After this less than encouraging beginning, Mother Teresa prayed with me for Alcoholics Anonymous and for all those suffering from substance addictions. She repeated to me what she had written Father Sam Ciccolini at the Interval Brotherhood in Akron, Ohio, many years before: "When I look into the eyes of an addict I see one of the more distressing disguises of our Lord Jesus." To discover blessing in the distressed and to discover Jesus in disguise is what Mother Teresa taught those who came to learn with open minds and broken— or at least breakable—hearts. After our prayer session, she asked us to come along and visit her orphanage. Upon entering a large room crowded with cribs, I witnessed firsthand her extraordinary charisma at work. The babies reached for her, and she met their open arms with hugs. She stopped at each crib just long enough to let her darshan overshadow each child; even the sleeping babes smiled. This woman was not only a spiritual force but a mother simply enjoying her children. Then, unexpectedly, she stopped, lifted a little boy high above her head, winked mischievously at my companion, and handed him the child. "Here, you take this one," she said laughing. "He needs a good home." Just like that!

Bim's friend was in shock. He had already adopted two of Mother's children and was separated from his wife; he had no plans to increase his family. He was wealthy enough but not a Catholic or even a Christian. This made no sense to me. Later on, when I met up with the American women volunteers, I asked them, "How do you deal with all these contradictions?" I asked, "Here is one of the most generous, compassionate women in the world—a woman who seldom if ever proselytizes, a woman who has said that working with the Sisters of Charity makes better Hindus out of Hindus, better Christians out of Christians, and better Moslems out of Moslems, and yet she discriminates against Protestants, divorced people, and whole countries based on her narrow interpretation of Christian doctrine?" Exasperated, I went on to tell them that, as we were leaving the orphanage, one of the young sisters had come running after us pleading, "No, no, you cannot have this baby; this baby not belong to us. We only babysit for his mother. His mother is working in town." (You can imagine how relieved my friend was!) I asked these women how Mother could give away the wrong child. They laughed, and one of them said, "Listen, Dagmar, Mother is not perfect! She is just a saint!" In the many years since, I've thought of that moment often, especially on Mother's Day. We don't have to be perfect—just saints, just willing to love one more child, one more day, one more time, for the time being. As Mother Teresa said, "God does not expect us to do great things perfectly, just little things with great love."

· · ·

In the early 1960s, the State Department considered India to be a "hardship post." I could never understand that. Granted, the climate took some adjusting to, with the incredibly dry, hot summers followed by the unbelievably humid monsoon season. But the winter and early spring months were almost perfect. Cool, sunny days and clear blue skies greeted us every day. We had beautifully furnished living quarters,(with air conditioning) and a club complete with swimming pool, tennis courts, and PX shopping facilities where we could buy almost anything tax-free while the government took care of all shipping costs to and from the post. We also had free health care. But most amazing of all, everyone had servants to help with the children, the household, the laundry, the garden, the cooking, the driving—you name it. All of us lived better in India than we would have ever been able to live in the United States. Still, many Americans, especially many of the foreign service wives, were incessantly complaining about their servants and were very critical of India and her people.

There were some notable exceptions, like Kitty Green, the wife of our deputy chief of mission. She loved and respected Indians, and it was she who introduced me to volunteering with Mother Teresa. For some of my time in India I worked part time as a music teacher at the Playhouse School, a private nursery and kindergarten owned and operated by the Nanda sisters.

And for almost our whole first year, we were house parents at the American International School boarding unit. The teenagers of diplomats from all over Asia were housed in this boarding school so they could attend the American International School in New Delhi. Most of them were spoiled and quite unruly, which is why the original professional teaching staff quit one day without even giving the ambassador notice. So Chet asked us to reside temporarily in the school. Since Dick continued to spend most of his time working at the embassy, I was the one who became responsible for those twenty-some teenagers—and, of course, my eight-month-old son. My life was hectic, but at least it was never boring. Maybe it was because the kids felt compassion for us, who were also displaced, or maybe they just had an easier time identifying with us than with the previous house parents. Whatever the reason, we seldom had major problems. Once, though, some of the boys stole the flag from the top of the Chinese embassy—a stupid move at any time but especially back then, when the U.S. didn't even have diplomatic relations with China. If those kids had been caught, God only knows what trouble we could have been in. And returning the flag proved almost as risky as stealing it in the first place. But in the end it all worked out.

My days in India were fairly predictable. I got up early with Eric, had a massage, and prepared the house for that evening's guests or made plans to spend the evening with friends. I then drove to Playhouse School and, once a week, accompanied Kitty to the orphanage. Many of my closest friends lived in the same area, and much of our time was spent visiting with each other. Of course, food shopping was a challenge all over again. Everything had to be found in open markets. What I liked least about shopping was buying chickens, which had to be killed right before my very eyes to make sure they were fresh. Still, I much preferred being a housewife in New Delhi than in New Haven.

I also became very good at bargaining. My Indian middle-class women friends spent even more time shopping than did most American women. The difference was they did much of it at home. The jeweler came to their houses with gems, and the women designed and created their own ornaments. The tailor brought an array of fabrics and was able to copy almost any pattern from fashion magazines. The skill of Indian craftsmen is extraordinary. Kashmiri carpet wallahs regularly stopped by, as did sari vendors from Banares. The exquisite richness of the wares and the Indian way of marketing them was very seductive and effective.

Dick and I did a great deal of informal entertaining. We befriended painters, writers, musicians, government officials, and diplomats from all over the world. We traveled a great deal, too, because when Chet and Steb traveled together they almost always wanted us to join them. They treated us to extended vacations in Kulu, Kashmir, Bhutan, and Kerela. The life we were leading in India could hardly be considered a hardship. Never again was life better.

The only drawback throughout it all was that I was usually pregnant. Neither the Pill nor the IUD prevented me from becoming pregnant. Even though I was still happy to add children to our little family, being pregnant in New Delhi was especially difficult because of the heat and perpetual hustle and bustle of the nonstop socializing. But the Medical Mission Sisters at Holy Family Hospital were great nurses, and giving birth in Delhi was more relaxed than it had been back home. My ob/gyn was a woman who, after helping me deliver Christopher, got pregnant herself. The measure of her humility and wisdom became clear when she asked me to coach her through this experience, since, according to her, I really knew birthing while she had only witnessed it thus far.

Sometime during my first pregnancy in India, my mother and her best friend Gerti Grobauer came to visit from Vienna. Schlange, as we called her, had the most amazing body—always tanned and slim. She had long, never-ending legs and large, firm breasts. However, my dumpy, pregnant insecurities over having her in the house were matched by her own inferiority complex. She had divorced her husband a few years before that visit because he had been unfaithful to her with some of his students. After the divorce, she discovered that finding men was easy enough with her looks, but finding one who would be true was impossible. When it came to married men, she was almost pathological. She tested them all and then detested them for succumbing to her charm. She was in her early thirties, somewhere between my mother's age and mine, and therefore was friends with both of us. Despite all I knew about her, I trusted her to respect my home and marriage. But she did not. My mother confronted her and accused her of attempting to seduce Dick. I wanted to believe the best, but Mutti told me that if I didn't kick Schlange out, she would leave on the next flight back to Vienna. I resented the ultimatum and refused to make a choice. Fortunately, Schlange chose to leave, and I never saw her again. The next year she killed herself while driving her car at a senseless speed.

When I recall Schlange's story after all these years, I realize how hard it still is for women to be self-confident enough to trust each other. I did not trust my mother; I could not trust my friend; worst of all, I could not trust my own instincts. In all the fights and finger-pointing, however, the one person none of us blamed was Dick. Here was a young, promising diplomat married less than two years, with a one-year-old son and another baby on the way, who was willing to risk it all for just another sexual conquest. First, he claimed that my mother was imagining things, and then he simply accused Schlange of attempting to seduce him. This incident demonstrated that my husband's inability to stay faithful and his unwillingness to be truthful were traits he brought into our marriage, and his problem was matched by my determination to avoid confronting it. So, while India was my first true home away from home, India was also the place where our marriage was first tested and failed.

Life did return to "normal." I gave birth to Christopher that April of 1965. From the very start, he was nothing like his brother. Eric was blond and had a sunny, open disposition; Christopher had dark curls and sad eyes. He was more attached to me and seemed to need continuous reassurance and praise. Christopher was also accident prone. He tried to do whatever Eric did, and that usually meant he was in way over his head. He ran too fast and tripped, he jumped into the swimming pool before he could swim, and he tried to catch animals that were better left alone, such as poisonous snakes. He was fearless and very affectionate. Christopher still has two fully developed sides to his personality—the one that believes he can do anything and the one that imagines that anything that could go wrong will go wrong in his life. I was very happy with those two boys but admit that, when I found myself expecting again the following year, I did wish for a girl.

When labor pains began at around noon on October 18, 1966, I was at a hairdresser in the middle of Old Delhi. By the time Dick picked me up, my contractions were less than five minutes apart. We set off to Holy Family Hospital. Rush hour in New York City is tame compared to Old Delhi at noon. Suddenly, in the midst of bullock carts and a wild assortment of rickshaws and bicycles, our car stalled. I was too focused on breathing through the contractions to care, but Dick was beside himself. Though he was never much of a mechanic, that important day he rose to the occasion and miraculously managed to get us moving again.

When we arrived at the hospital, a nurse tried to stop him from coming into the delivery room with me, probably because he was covered with red dust and sweat from the ordeal. But, as he is fond of telling the story, he was bigger than the nurse, and he knew I wanted him at my side more than ever. He announced to this diminutive Indian woman, "If you think you can stop me from being present at the birth of my child, just try!"

Once I was on the delivery table, everything seemed to stop. A deep silence descended on me, and I began to doubt there was a baby to be born at all. I felt nothing. The phone rang, and I heard someone give directions to set up some patient transport. More silence. I felt myself beginning to slip. "What happened to the baby?" Dick did not hear my question. The phone rang again, and I overheard the same conversation: "She is almost ready for the transport." I asked Dick, "Who is almost ready for the transport?" Again, he heard nothing. He kept caressing my arm and murmuring assurances that all was going just fine. I began to sink, feeling lost in this vast world of birthing. I thought I was in grave danger, despite the fact that everything and everybody around me seemed calm and untroubled. Then slowly my body woke from what felt like underwater slumber. A gentle trembling began to spread from deep inside me, and I knew I had made it into transition without struggling through labor. When Maria Gabriella emerged—IUD and all!—it was clear she was ready to take on the world.

Right from the start, Gabriella was the most determined of the Celeste children. Unlike Christopher, she seemed to navigate efficiently. She, too, tried hard to keep up with her older siblings, but at the same time she had a very strong sense of herself. I always trusted her and depended on her sense of justice. As a grown woman, I believe she will always succeed, because, like her father, she cares little about credit and knows how to leverage resources for results. Her kindness and generosity of heart and her willingness to share herself are inspiring. Maria Gabriella is a fascinating blend of tough and gentle. She is fiercely loyal and critical at the same time. She has an exquisite sense of fair play and is not afraid to acknowledge her mistakes; when she apologizes, she means it and then moves on. She is a born leader and perhaps the one destined to follow her father into public life someday. Gabriella is also a deeply spiritual woman. The year her grandfather Celeste died, she decided to go to India to work with Mother Teresa. When she returned home she told us, "the first man I helped to die had grandpa's eyes, and from then on I understood what Mother Teresa was trying to teach when she insisted on recognizing Jesus in all those we served." She has the rare gift of true presence, and her empathy is honest and capable of consoling even the most despairing souls.

By the time we returned to Ohio in 1967, anything seemed possible. We were blessed with a deepened faith in our abilities to build a better world and with three wonderful children. I believed that Dick and I must have been doing something right. Doesn't the Gospel assure us "you shall know them by their fruits"?

"I want to see Ohio be the best"

Cliffs that rise a thousand feet without a break
Lake that stretches a hundred miles without a wave
Trees that for twenty thousand years your vows have kept
You have suddenly healed the pain of the traveler's heart
And moved his brush to write a new song.
—*Chan Iang-Sheng*

Lakewood, Ohio
November 21, 1995
Presentation of Mary

This week, our son Christopher and his wife, Melanie, embarked on one of life's more arduous adventures: the purchase of a new house. It reminded me of how important home is, that places—perhaps even more than people—are an integral part of personal transformations. Each of the houses Dick and I remodeled and each of the many homes we created in our thirty-plus years together revealed aspects of ourselves, our marriage, and our time. Each place I lived in became a sacred space for me and my loved ones to grow in. I believe that every place we chose also chose us and became an essential piece in the pattern of our lives.

How did it happen that three decades later I find myself in the same community—even on the same street, Lake Avenue—as where we settled in our first house. I sometimes wonder if this will be my last home, or if maybe someday one of my fondest dreams will come true and I will somehow, somewhere build a house of my own. Then again, I might yet make good on our common dream to develop the ten acres surrounding Himmelblau House into TYRIAN, a community of friends and artists where simplicity, creativity, and diversity can flourish. Or, as I grow older, I might move in with one of my children, or perhaps more of my kids will move closer to me. I wonder how many more places I will live before I find eternal rest in that small cemetery on Kelley's Island.

In the process of our divorcing, Himmelblau, the family homestead, became an unexpected bone of contention. Initially, I was willing to let it go, *provided I could get some assurance that our children and I would be able to continue to use it and that our children and their children would inherit it one day. At the time, I reasoned that Dick knew better how to care for it and, most importantly, had sufficient financial resources to continue proper upkeep and make future improvements; I didn't think I was capable of maintaining the property and was most unsure of my financial future.*

Since Dick could not afford to pay me the full value of the property, I suggested that he offer me two of the lots closest to the lake. He not only rejected such a compromise but also refused to commit to bequeathing Himmelblau to our children. It was then that I realized we had arrived at a crossroads. Himmelblau was purchased with the help of our respective parents, whose intention it was to benefit their children and grandchildren. I could have accepted the two back lots RFC offered, even the ridiculously low payment, but relinquishing our children's right to inherit the place seemed cruel and unfair. So I countered Dick's offer for no more and no less than what he had put on the table. I have never regretted that decision, and I hope that together with the help of friends and children, we will keep Himmelblau House for many more generations.

Himmelblau is sacred space. On the shore of Lake Erie, facing the sunrise, surrounded by fire lilies and fossil-encrusted stone messengers, the house has withstood the battering of many a ferocious northeastern windstorm to provide shelter and healing energy. Himmelblau is dedicated to the dark, native, pregnant Mother of Guadalupe. Dick and I built her a little shrine at the base of a large black walnut tree that grows near the lake's edge. I believe the simple act of building that shelter for Mary transformed our ordinary summer home into a secret sanctuary, where She lives as Maiden, Mother, and Crone and manifests Herself in cedar groves, white roses, poppies, prairie wildflowers, and rock gardens. Just recently, renowned Ohio artist Linda Apple finished carving a healing totem on a still-rooted dead tree on the Himmelblau grounds. Facing west are the seven chakras and Hermes's staff; facing east is the beautiful lace of the tree's spirit; and on the north and south are the wings that transform this Hermes totem into an Angel of healing.

To the ancient Greeks, Hermes was the traveler, the messenger, the one who transported souls to Hades, the mischievous thief. But he was also the ruler of dreams, and, with the help of his staff, the bearer of true happiness and good fortune.

Hermes was supposed to be the inventor of language, and this not merely on verbal grounds. He is hermeneus ("interpreter"), a linguistic mediator. By nature he is the begetter and bringer of something light-like, a clarifier. This God of exposition and interpretation seeks and in his spirit . . . is led forward to the deepest mystery. Like [St.] Anthony, he is the designated bearer of divine children. He also is God of the vineyards on the island of Lesbos. Like with [St.] Francis, Hermetic spiritual aspects exist in friendly union with the divine-animal aspect. Like Jesus, Hermes is believed to bring light into darkness. Whoever does not shy away from the dangers of the most profound depths and the newest pathways, which Hermes is always prepared to open, may follow him and reach out to all. For those to whom life is an adventure—whether an adventure of love or of spirit or both—he is the common guide.[1]

Through Hermes, every house becomes an opening and a point of departure to the paths that lead away into the distance.

One early morning in 1984, I heard an inner voice telling me that Hermes was my beloved inner man. Since then, I have taken Hermes to be my soul partner, my most secret and mysterious anam cara. I believe that the tree spirit who emerged under Linda's skilled hands is both Hermes and Raphael, and with their help and guidance—and that of saints ancestors—we will continue to creatively leverage the Braun-Celeste legacy. Through TYRIAN[2] we will create a network strong enough to continue

---

1. Karl Kerenyi, *Hermes, Guide of Souls: Mythologem of the Masculine Source of Life* (Spring Publications, 1986).

2. TYRIAN is a nonprofit educational network, a learning community of artists and friends dedicated to the pursuit of creativity and peace. See www.tyrian.net.

to grow Himmelblau into a sanctuary filled with joy and peace for our whole extended terrestrial and celestial tribe.

. . .

When I stand on my balcony high above Lake Avenue, I can see the sun rise and set over the lively waves of the same great lake that links my place of solitude in Lakewood to our place of togetherness on the island. I can feel the same wind and see clouds that in a short time may rain on both places. I can see the many trees of Lakewood and the skyline of Cleveland, the gateway to my American journey and to the testing ground of my soul. Next year Cleveland will celebrate its two-hundredth birthday and Himmelblau will turn one hundred and Vienna will celebrate one thousand years of existence. Today, just two days away from my own fifty-fifth birthday, I wonder if I will ever feel truly at home in any of these places.

I trust that my willingness to navigate my own transitions gracefully will in some small way give me courage for the journey. I'm reminded of a plaque Stephen brought home one day: "Home is where the heart is." At this time in my life I have come to believe that "home is where the heart feels free." Free enough to grow wings and joyful enough to burst into song. Learning to hear my own heart-song without the harmonizing voice of my spouse is a challenge. But who knows who might yet come along and join the chorus in days to come? Maybe home is simply where we improvise and harmonize with whoever shows up.

A fter we returned from India in 1967, we decided to buy a house of our own. We wanted to live near the lake yet still in the city. With the generous help of Chet Bowles and my father, we were able to afford the $2,500 down payment. To be able to buy our own house at the start of our family life together seemed almost miraculous.

I love and respect the art of designing and building houses almost as much as the art of politics. One of the many things I loved best about Dick was that he seemed to be an expert at both: he's a good politician and a gifted historian, but he's also a competent carpenter. So when we decided to remodel our home on Lake Avenue, we did it with the help of Will Trout, a most creative Cleveland architect, and Dick did much of the reconstruction work himself.

Our home was a simple Midwest frame house situated across from Edgewater Park. The neighborhood was relatively quiet and the homes were well maintained; a small Lutheran church was located just down the street (and I discovered, to my surprise, that services were still celebrated in German). But while our front yard was a essentially a park, our back yard was a wasteland. One of the first things my mother did when she came to visit was help me to landscape. I still remember my awe at her strength as she dug and pulled out fully grown bushes all around the property and replaced them with plants that would yield either flowers or food. Plants that were just "green stuff" had to go, she said. But the very best part of this house was that we could see the lake from almost every room in the house. I'm certain that landscape does make a difference to the well-being of body, mind, and soul and that communities and cultures flourish when they settle along great bodies of water. After all, nothing can grow without being watered. I was born and raised along the banks of the majestic Danube and enjoyed summers by the Adriatic, so it was in keeping that I now live on the shores of this great lake.

Setting up a houschold has always helped me grow deeper roots into a community and simultaneously into the ground of my own being. So it was soon after settling in that we began establishing ties within the larger West Side community. I became a member of St. Coleman's parish and a founding member of the Community of Saint Malachi. I was a volunteer assistant teacher at the Urban Community School and served on the board of the West Side Ecumenical Ministry, and Dick became president of CRASH (Citizens Revolt Against Substandard Housing). We both joined the Ward Club, and I started work with the Louisa May Alcott PTA. I started making friends, too. Through the PTA I met Anda Cook and Carol Stringer, who remain near and dear to this day. And it was about this time that Alicia Miller, my first female friend in America, and her husband, Bill, moved to Edgewater Drive, bringing with them architect Tom Zung and his wife, Carol, to remodel their home. They, too, became close friends.

In our new home, we set about celebrating old and devising new feasts and rituals for family and friends. It was then that Christmas became a particularly festive time for us. We invited people to celebrate Advent with us, have cookies, sing carols, and share in the wonderfilled tension of waiting for the birth of the Christ Child. The 1969 season was made extra-special with the Christmas Eve birth of our daughter Maria Teresa Noelle, who waited patiently to appear until after I'd finished all the baking and cooking and wrapping. Dick and I named her Maria Theresa, after the Austrian empress who perfected the art of peace keeping, and Alicia called her Noelle. She was baptized at St. Coleman's, where Father Haas was the pastor. It was Father Haas who first encouraged me to take on more public responsibilities by nominating me for the Diocesan Ecumenical Commission and appointing me parish representative to the West 65th Cluster of the West Side Ecumenical Ministry. I soon became aware of how much poverty surrounded us and helped create the first Hunger Center in that area by involving the churches in our cluster.

It was a person, not a party or a cause, however, who had first converted me from watching politics to working at it. Dick Celeste's enthusiasm for the cause of peace enlivened much of our early courtship. That passion for peace, as much as anything else about him, persuaded me to choose him as my partner for life. Anyone who cared about the common good so deeply and had the good sense to temper idealism with pragmatism and common sense with compassion was not only trustworthy but was bound to become a leader. I have to admit that when I joined my life in love to his, my hopes were wild and my expectations high. I wanted not only to create a healthier and more serene home for myself and my future children than the one I was raised in, but I also felt called to bring about a safer, saner, and sounder world. Nothing has affected my personal consciousness more than participating in American democratic politics—not only in the politics of anti-racism and peace but especially the feminist politics of passion and partnership.

Reflecting back on those early days in Cleveland helps me realize with gratitude how God had been preparing us for the leadership challenges ahead. In later years, it was only natural for us to contribute the profits of our first inaugural to the Ohio Hunger Task Force and those of the second celebration to the Homeless Coalition. My dedication as First Lady to such issues as day care, domestic violence, recovery, peace and conflict management, and Holocaust education originated from very close personal experiences with each of those issues. Right from the start of our personal and political partnership, Dick and I were guided by our higher power to use our brief moment in history to reach out to those most in need. With thousands of other Ohioans, we shared the privilege of moving Ohio toward healthier times and together became a "constituency for change with conscience."

My first campaign was the historic battle in 1967 to elect Carl Stokes the first black mayor of Cleveland—and the first black mayor in North America. The battle was personal and the outcome painful for the Celeste family. Frank Celeste had been a very popular Democratic mayor of Lakewood, a very Republican suburb of Cleveland. He was the first, and for many years the only, Democrat elected to that office. Just like Dick, Frank had a knack for bringing people together. His first mayoral election was nonpartisan, with the citizens of Lakewood disregarding party labels by electing him. After that election, the Republican Party convinced the voters to change the city charter back to partisan elections. Despite such maneuvers, Frank Celeste was reelected and served with such distinction that his legacy continues to empower Lakewood Democrats to this day. He voluntarily left the office because he was convinced that no one should serve more than eight years in any elected office. While mayor of Lakewood, he built a new city hall, improved municipal parks and recreation programs, returned Lakewood Hospital to fiscal soundness, and developed the Barton Center, the first senior citizen housing facility in the country.

Carl Stokes, a young black legislator, had come close to winning the office of mayor of Cleveland in the previous election. Knowing this, Cleveland's establishment decided to offer financial and other support to Frank Celeste simply to defeat Carl. Disregarding advice from Dick, who was then far away in India, not to get into the race without Carl's support, Frank accepted the challenge to run. After he entered the race, the Democratic incumbent, Ralph Locher, decided to stand for reelection after all. So now the same folks who had talked Frank into getting in the race were trying to get him out. But Frank stayed his ground, and he was crushed at the polls. Rather than being respected for rejecting bribes and withstanding the clumsy and brutal assaults by the most reactionary elements of the Democratic Party power elite, Frank came in third and was accused by every racist in town of having been part of a plot to divide the white vote in order to give Carl Stokes a clear ride to City Hall.

As much as Frank Celeste's reputation in Lakewood helped Dick win his first primary and general elections in 1970, his father's campaign for mayor of Cleveland had turned white Democrats and Republicans into bitter Celeste foes. Frank Celeste was a man ahead of his time, and despite his many private failings, it was his effort as much as anything else that paved the way for his son's political rise. Frank's dream, true to his immigrant roots, was to see his son become the first Italian-American president. He did not live to see that day, but by the time he died in 1988 his dreams had changed. By then his greatest triumph and joy was to have lived long enough to see and know his great-granddaughter, Eleanor.

After the primary, I worked hard every day at the Stokes headquarters (even though I was pregnant with Noelle). I liked Carl, respected his wife, Shirley, and was overjoyed when we won. The Stokes victory was an amazing political happening—not only for black people in Cleveland but for people of color and goodwill everywhere across the nation—and proved that the black community had become strong and sophisticated enough to elect one of its own and that a growing number of white people were ready to overcome traditional racial prejudices. Carl Stokes's win suggested to me that what we call charisma in politics is simply sex appeal. Over the years many claimed to have slept with him, and he did eventually leave his family to marry a Scandinavian beauty queen. But he was a good mayor and over time served with distinction in many other public positions. He was a great strategist, and together with his brother Louis he consolidated the power of the black community in the Twenty-first Congressional District.

• • •

Cleveland was home to us for more than a decade. By the time Natalie was born on Father's Day 1971, we had to expand into the third floor of our Lake Avenue home to accommodate our ever-increasing family. The children grew to love Cleveland; they even enjoyed the challenge of busing, because for the first time they had the opportunity to really make friends with children of diverse social, economic, and racial backgrounds. The move to our new home, the Governor's Residence, in 1983, however, presented more than a few challenges.

It was later, while at Yale, that Noelle wrote her senior thesis in American Studies: "When Your Home Is a Fish Bowl." She interviewed other young people who had grown up in political families about the numerous advantages and disadvantages of life in the public eye. I was intrigued by the idea of home as a fish bowl—beautiful to look at but restrictive and exposed for all to see. To most outsiders, the public nature of political life seems to be the harshest aspect of that calling.

It was surprising to me how most of us came to enjoy this form of almost exhibitionist existence. Perhaps precisely because the personal is so political, and because the private is likely to become so public, public servants have to learn not only to overproject their positive assets but—most damaging of all—to hide their shadows even from themselves. Furthermore, to be ready to perform at all times politicians learn to value potency over empathy. Their ability to be available to their loved ones decreases as their desire to be available to others increases. Their ever-growing capacity to influence the destiny of the people diminishes their willingness to reflect honestly and thoughtfully on their own lives, their own relationships.

After Geraldine Ferraro became the first woman vice presidential nominee—as well as the first VP candidate to be blamed for her party's defeat—she told me, "If I had ever suspected the price my family would have to pay for my day in the sun, I could have never justified it. Thank God I was kept in the dark." I agree. While the most lasting memories of my time in the fish bowl are the good ones, if I had known the price the children and I would have to pay for Dick's day in the sun, I don't believe I would have been able to participate.

The first week after Dick's victory over Jim Rhodes, Helen Rhodes called and graciously offered to show me the Residence; it remains a long-standing tradition for the outgoing First Lady to take the new First Lady on a tour of the Mansion. Helen welcomed me warmly. As we went from room to room, she described some of the problems in the Residence. Many of the rooms had not been occupied in years. The shades were down, curtains were drawn, most beds had old mildewed mattresses on them. When we tried to switch on lights, more often than not the bulbs had burned out. Every one of the rooms needed to be disinfected, cleaned, and painted, not to mention decorated. As we wandered around, I also realized that except for what later became the "meditation room," there was not a single bookshelf in the thirty-some-room house. Helen thought that there might have been some shelves in the living room originally, but they had been paneled over. I wondered what we would do with the thousands of books Dick and I had collected. (For if Dick and I ever had a common avocation, it was buying books!) I was overwhelmed by the task that loomed ahead, but also exhilarated by the sheer size and raw beauty of this grand house.

At the end of the tour, Helen and I settled in the living room to chat, valiantly attempting to ignore the photographers snapping away and the TV reporters discreetly waiting in the foyer. I wanted advice. This woman across from me had served as First Lady of Ohio longer than any other woman in Ohio's history, and despite it all she had kept her family intact. I knew I might never get another chance to learn from her. I began by asking her to tell me about her favorite times in this house. She softened and opened up to reminisce about her daughter's wedding and picnics with her grandchildren and to complain about all the politicos who holed up in her kitchen until the middle of the night.

Encouraged, I decided to ask for some more personal advice. "What do I need to watch out for? What do you wish someone had warned you about when you became First Lady of Ohio?" She looked at me thoughtfully and said, "Well, the best advice I can think of giving you, Dagmar, is simply this: Don't ever let them put you in a receiving line in your own home." I was not sure I understood what I heard and must have shown my puzzlement. "See that spot over there?" she continued, pointing beyond the living room toward the foyer. "Right there in front of the dining room doors—that's where I stood for days on end, hour after hour, receiving well-wishers from all over the state. It began right with the inaugural and never seemed to stop. Finally my back gave out. You may wonder why we put that hideous indoor/outdoor carpet right over the beautiful slate tiles? Because my back could not take standing on that hard, uncarpeted stone floor any longer, and Jim did not want to spend too much on the Mansion." I looked at that spot and almost could see Helen in her younger days, shaking one hand after the other and smiling while hiding the pain shooting from her legs up her spine. I thought it sad that Helen Rhodes did not have many fond memories of the Mansion, which was no doubt why she refused to return to it when Rhodes was reelected to his third term.

I remember another First Lady who was not too happy in that house. The first time I met Kate Gilligan was in 1970 at a reception for newly elected legislators. Jack Gilligan had won the governor's race, and Dick had won his first campaign as state representative to the then 49th Ohio House District, which at the time was comprised of Cleveland's First Ward and all of Lakewood. There was a lot to celebrate in Ohio that year. When we entered the Mansion, Jack and Katie Gilligan were in a receiving line welcoming their guests. As I shook the First Lady's hand, I congratulated her. "Seems like you enjoy politics," she said with a weary smile playing in her eyes. "I do. I love campaigning," I gushed. "Well, that's nice, Dagmar," she replied, "I don't!" and that was the end of the conversation. That was not the end of our relationship, however; we later campaigned together when Dick aspired to become Jack Gilligan's lieutenant governor. Katie was a quiet, humble woman, and her many pursuits to better the lives of mentally ill people seldom, if ever, put her in the spotlight. Even though she disliked politics, she did love people and served Ohioans very well.

Helen's advice and Katie's resigned tone haunted me, and I was determined that I would transform that sorry Mansion into a Residence full of magic and joyful memories. I was grateful to both my predecessors, because without their honest warning I might have done as told, stood in receiving lines, officiated at countless boring receptions, and never chosen to set my own course and draw up a new set of guidelines to benefit myself and maybe a few future First Ladies. But despite my determination to become the happiest First Lady of them all, the house won. Some think it's cursed. Who knows?

When we emerged from the living room, Helen and I were surrounded by the press. They asked Helen what she had told me about the house. And she simply said, "The truth." Of course, they wanted to know what "truth" she was referring to. She shot back, "That this is a most difficult place to maintain. It is drafty and humid, dark and intimidating, even the roof leaks."

One of the reporters asked, "Why didn't you do something about it?"

"Me? Why don't you ask the ex-governor of Ohio?"

I was stunned. So were the reporters there that day. But I was also pleasantly surprised. This was no shrinking violet; she knew who she was and was wise enough not to claim too much power or relieve her favorite governor of his responsibility to face the consequences of his poor stewardship.

Neither Governor Gilligan nor Governor Rhodes had given much thought to the Residence. Gilligan spent considerable effort in renovating the official offices of the governor and the cabinet room in the statehouse, and Rhodes spent just as much effort in restoring them to his favorite red-white-and-blue color scheme. Furthermore, since the Rhodes family did not live in the Residence during his third term, he let the house and garden go to hell.

So, by the time we moved in, the place had been abandoned and abused for almost eight years. To make matters worse, it had been rented out for free on a first-come-first-served basis for weddings, bar mitzvahs, and other large events. The one staff person on the grounds, Obie, was expected to keep it all together, an impossible task. A former prison inmate who had been pardoned many years ago by Governor Rhodes, Obie was like an indentured servant—at the beck and call of the governor day and night. He lived in the carriage house amid broken furniture and dirty clothes. I was told that his wife at the time, Mildred, and some of her kids periodically stayed on the third floor of the Mansion. But all that changed when we moved in. We told Obie and Mildred that, like any other state employee, they would work a proper shift, be able to take vacations, and no longer be allowed to live on the premises. In time, Obie came to appreciate having a life of his own again; but Mildred never got used to us. Obie continued in his position for more than four years, and we all truly valued his gentle manner and commitment to hard work.

It was a few days after my initial viewing of the Residence with Helen Rhodes that Alicia Miller and I went back for a more in-depth assessment of the challenge ahead of us. Alicia had volunteered to take charge of finding the right architect and helping us transform the moth-balled Mansion into a Residence worthy of the great State of Ohio. The plaster was falling in most rooms; the wallpaper had dried up and was peeling off the walls. The mattresses smelled of urine and had to be dumped; some of the carpets were rotted. Not a single shower worked, and the toilet in the master bedroom was beyond repair. The house was infested with rats, and the upstairs bathrooms were crawling with silverfish. The wood floors needed repairing, and the slate floors required refinishing. All the electrical wiring had to be replaced. And after we moved in, more damage became apparent: the plumbing, heating, and air-conditioning systems had been patched up for years, and we also eventually found the money to reslate the roof, a project that Governor George Voinovich saw through to completion.

We were able to accomplish only a few things before we officially moved in. On the second floor were the master bedroom and study, bedrooms for the children, a family room, and, later, a guest room. Across from the master bedroom and study was a tiny room. It had no closet but did have the only bookshelves in the house. A large leaded glass window and a door leading to a balcony overlooking the garden took up one whole side of the room—all in all, three walls of books and one wall of glass. No room for a bed. It was beautiful but seemingly useless.

I sat for a long time in the empty room, wondering what to make of it—in fact, what to make of my life as First Lady of Ohio. The Scripture passage that kept coming to my mind was the one about the "lilies of the fields," and a voice deep inside me said softly, "See! I am providing for you always. Just be still and know I am. Tomorrow will take care of itself. Trust I am taking care of you day by day." From then on, I used the little room as a meditation/prayer space. It eventually housed my inspirational books, a hand-carved Madonna that a Lithuanian delegation had brought as their inaugural gift, my special crucifix from Austria, and other very personal, precious objects that lent themselves to peaceful contemplation. There were to be no phones or even music there. Whenever I wanted to have a quiet conversation with my spouse, one of the kids, staff, or special friends, we would go to the meditation room. There, more than anywhere else, the fish bowl felt more like a nest.

We visualized the third floor as future office space; but when I ventured up there by elevator, I had quite a time finding my way back. Most of the lights had burned out, the back stairs were barricaded, and every one of the eight or so rooms and closets was filled with junk: discarded papers, old calling cards and stationery, torn books, wedding invitations for one or another of the Rhodes kids, clothes, curtains, broken lamps, and so on. But we had to sift through all of this by hand, because every once in a while we hit upon a piece of state silver, an antique book, or an oriental rug that had been cleaned, rolled up, and stashed away in some remote corner. It took Dick two weeks of sorting to go through it all before we could remove two truckloads of trash.

Furthermore, unknown to us, the phone lines were labeled with phone numbers that had been disconnected years before. The first night we stayed at the Residence, we had no food in the house, so Dick called to order pizza. When asked where to deliver it, he proudly said, "to the Governor's Residence, please." When asked for a phone number to verify the order, Dick gave the number on the phone in his hand. An hour later, there was still no pizza, so he called back and was told, "Well, I called that number and it's been disconnected, so we thought it was just a prank."

That first night I was overwhelmed and bewildered. The house was enormous! I tried to sleep but was too tired and too excited. I decided to slip out of the master suite and make my way to the kitchen for a cup of tea. When I switched on the light, I saw the whole floor move! Roaches scurried into the woodwork. But left in the kitchen, stunned by the sudden bright light, was a small rat (or a huge mouse).

Eventually the proud Residence emerged from the old Mansion and became a home. For eight years the whole extended family, including spouses of loved ones and friends, came together to celebrate and share memorable times. At first, however, Gabriella chose to stay in Cleveland to finish her last year at Magnificat High School. We had leased the Lake Avenue house for very little to the Sisters of Saint Joseph, and they in turn let Gabriella keep her room until she graduated. The rest of the kids packed up their stuff and moved to Columbus; but since Christopher and Eric were, respectively, at Stanford and Yale, it was really only Noelle, Natalie, and Stephen who were home all the time during those eight years. In 1983, the same year we moved in, Eric met Mary Hess at Yale. After they graduated, they came to live with us at the Residence. Eric had decided to earn a master's degree in library science at Kent State University and Mary had started working on my staff. In 1988 they were married at the Newman Center, with the reception at the Residence. But the first Celeste wedding at the Residence was Christopher and Melanie's, in 1987. Their on-again/off-again relationship finally culminated in Melanie proposing on-stage at a Willie Nelson concert at the Ohio State Fair. A stunned Chris accepted, of course.

A state residence is a perfect example of how the public and private overlap. Creating within a public space a nest for a family requires vision and perseverance. Keeping the Residence open for official events during all the restoration activities was also a big a challenge. The first year was the hardest—we had to remodel the kitchen from top to bottom, including a waterlogged floor that jiggled when walked on. With the help of the Hubbard Company, which donated all the equipment, and Amish carpenters who built the cabinets that Bucchieri had designed, the end result was beautiful. We ended up with a large, professional kitchen that included a spacious family table and, of course, bookshelves. It was both efficient and cozy. I spent much of my time at that kitchen table, and so did many others, including the ever-vigilant state troopers who came in for coffee and company.

That first spring we realized there was no soil left in the gardens, as they had been neglected for years. Nothing but annuals had been planted in peat moss summer after summer. So to grow perennials, we had to truck in fresh soil. Early that spring, when a very ancient and mysterious-looking man paid me a visit, I also learned that the Residence had one of the oldest rose gardens in the country. He introduced himself as the president of the Rosarian Association and proceeded to tell me that our rose garden was older than that of the White House. He warned me that, unless restored, the roses would die. He offered his help, and that spring he dug up all the roses, cleaned their roots, and replanted them in fresh soil. He then explained to me that roses have to be trimmed down to branches that have five leaves in order for them to flourish. Is that why the Rosary is based on five decades? Perhaps some monk in the Middle Ages noted the magic of five in connection with roses. My Rosarian mentor lived long enough to save all the roses, and the following summer, shortly after the governor visited his state fair rose exhibit, our rose guardian passed on. Much of what I teach in my workshop, "The Mystery of the Blue Rose," is information he taught me, and I believe he still sends me clues now and then. Restoring the garden was a real challenge, but since gardening is one of the best stress healers, I greatly benefitted from that work. I don't think I would have ever learned to indulge in that pleasure had I not had the privilege of living for eight years in one of the grandest houses in Ohio supported by enough garden help to get the desert to bloom. Then again, maybe my love for gardens, especially the wilder variety, comes from my early childhood experiences of the wonderful orchards and vineyards of the Wachau.

At the time, I was an average gardener at best. In fact, even after eight years of practice designing the Residence gardens with the help of Nonni Casino and Bobbie Wiard, my practical skills seldom matched my vision. After visiting flower shows all over the world in preparation for Ameriflora, the first International Floral Exhibit in North America, I learned to transform my vision into reality and began to understand the importance of patience and preparation. Just as our whole life is influenced by our root experiences, so a garden is only as lush as the soil is fertile. Later, in my Columbus home on Pennsylvania Circle, I spent hours, sometimes days, selecting bargains from catalogs, only to end up buying my supplies at the local garden store on planting day. I might want a nice, clean expanse of ivy along the outside of our fence, only to discover that some bleeding hearts had chosen the semishade of the oak to naturalize in that very spot. I could, of course, transplant the bleeding hearts, but I might never see them again. If they found their way over there all by themselves, they must have had a good reason for it. As gardeners, we have to be wise enough to take such hints.

Once I began to work along with nature, I learned to become flexible. Just when I thought the planting plan was perfect, nature intervened; yet, if I tried to proceed without planning, weeds took over. Maybe nature is just like me—a good feminist. She wants both/and, not either/or—a gardener patient enough to plan and humble enough to change the soundest plan to accommodate her best surprises. So I learned to become a better partner with her, willing to do the work of planning and planting and wise enough to let her have her way, curiously awaiting her surprises season by season. The experience of our garden helped me become a better First Lady and a good enough mother and spouse.

Season by season the Residence gardens took shape. The perennial gardens, planted by Nonni the first year, were later enhanced by an award-winning herb garden designed by John Spofford, an artist from Athens, Ohio, and a new terrace to the side of the house was added with an entrance in the back. With the gardens more accessible, entertaining outside was easier, since people did not have to tramp through the house. We also installed large raised vegetable beds, and throughout the summers we were able to use our own produce and herbs and decorate the house with our own cut flowers. Furthermore, we surrounded the property with trees, both to hide a hideous chain-link fence and to gain some privacy. That first spring we also planted six (named for each of our children) redbud trees at the front of the house to protect the curtainless dining room from the curious. Finally, we surrounded the flag post in front of the Residence with wonderfully scented perennial red carnations, the official state flower of Ohio.

The Residence grounds were also used to install contemporary Ohio sculpture exhibits sponsored by the Ohio Arts Council. The only permanent installation was a piece donated to the residence by Alfred Tibor in memory of the children who died in the Holocaust, "so that all children will never forget." The piece represents a mother, father, and three children and is entitled "To Life!" At the request of the artist, a Holocaust survivor himself, we surrounded the sculpture with a minyan of apple trees.

Every three to six months, the Ohio Arts Council presented us with samples of works by Ohio contemporary artists, and Dick and I selected pieces we would enjoy living with, and the original art made the Residence a more vibrant place. Babs Sirak, a renowned art dealer and famed collector also helped with those initial selections. I've always thought that the simplest way to transform any space into a home is with original art. I'd much rather own an original work from an unknown artist than display the best reproductions of the most famous masters, for original art has a live voice and is capable of dialogue. Over the years, the Governor's Art Show became one of the more prestigious shows for emerging Ohio artists. We had the privilege to meet, and sometimes even befriend, the artists, and after such a personal connection their work spoke in even more surprising ways. I have never yet bought an original work of art without first getting to know the artist. To this day, I have saved all the catalogs the Ohio Arts Council designed for the residence shows, and in my more nostalgic moments I return to them and cherish the memory of those living works.

One of my favorite pieces is Nancy Crow's art quilt, *Contradictions*. Nancy once told me that quilting curved lines is much harder than any number of straight ones. *Contradictions* is all broken circles, a bit like a crazy version of the traditional double wedding band patterns. A synonym for "contradiction" is "denial," which is one of the many reasons I so admire this colorful, kaleidoscopic piece. I have come to realize that throughout those years at the Residence I lived submerged in deep denial; lulled by the beauty of the surroundings and the privilege of service, I never recognized the many ways our own wedding bands had been broken.

We had much help in financing all the renovations; private donors paid for most of the improvements. The rule was simple: any maintenance of the existing facility was paid for by the state; any improvement, such as the terrace and herb garden, was paid for by private donations. Columbus businessman Les Wexner agreed to chair the fund, and thanks to him and many others the necessary finances were always there. The first donation to what was to become the Friends of the Residence Fund came from Victor and Cookie Krupman, who gave enough money to replace the floor in the living room.

Steve Bucchieri was commissioned to design furniture for the Residence based on the architectural history and character of the house.

The house had some characteristics of Arts and Crafts, and the furnishings we chose were influenced by the designs of Charles Mackintosh, the Scottish architect who was the leader of the Art Nouveau movement. The furniture was built by Cleveland-area craftspeople. Because I didn't think we could find or afford to get expensive Ohio pieces that would be sturdy enough to accommodate the heavy use of an official residence, we thought well-built, historically referenced pieces would serve us better over time. I was saddened when George and Janet Voinovich chose not to honor the aesthetic and historical value of the pieces or the fine craftsmanship that went into constructing them. They have since removed the specially designed collection and replaced it with some "indigenous" antiques and new pieces decorated with carved buckeyes and cardinals. I only hope the original collection is stored safely at the Ohio Historical Society and that some future First Family will appreciate their beauty and comfort and enjoy them once again.

One of the most magnificent features of the Residence is its beautiful leaded-glass windows. Each room features a different design, and every window offers a perfectly delightful view. My favorite room by far was the smaller living room in the back of the house. It had windows on three of the four sides, a generous stone fireplace, and lush silver-gray velvet love seats. That room was a perfect place to enjoy a snowy afternoon watching cardinals and blue jays flit about the many strategically placed feeding stations. I spent many serene hours in that room. I remember with love the women in my theology circle who, month after month for almost seven years, gathered there to celebrate our faith, vision, and wisdom. I remember a quiet chat with Christa Wolf, the East German writer, and May Sarton, writer and lover of women. I remember the fun we had with Peter, Paul and Mary, Pete Seeger, Arlo Guthrie, Holly Near, Ronnie Gilbert, Jane Yolen, Maya Angelou, Lily Tomlin, Letty Pogrebin, Helen Caldicott, Gloria Steinem, Nikki Giovanni, and so many others. I remember numerous intimate moments with close friends snatched almost in secret late at night. And sometimes Dick and I would sit, just the two of us, and read or chat or simply share the silence of the dark, quiet house, interrupted only by the periodic rounds the troopers made as they checked the premises.

We also created opportunities for other artists to perform regularly at the Residence. Monthly chamber music in the magnificent music room overlooking the wide expanse of an ever-more luscious garden, poetry readings, and evenings dedicated to individual Ohio writers of the highest quality enriched our lives. The music evenings were coordinated by Sharon Mann Polk, who brought the finest Ohio musicians to perform at these occasions. She hosted the performances with an exquisite sense for the music and the genius of the composers and a subtle sense of humor.

But having sometimes hundreds of people flood into our lives every day was restrictive. The Residence was almost always in official use: regular public tours, special off-hour tours, work meetings for the cabinet and governor, lunches to highlight particular programs, award receptions, cocktail parties. Every department and many constituencies had access to the Residence. Our only rule was that no event could take place unless the Governor or the First Lady, or both, agreed to attend. This was quite a departure from the past, when much was happening in the house without the participation of the First Family. Also, any ambassador or head of state that came to Columbus was offered the residence guest rooms. I remember official dinners for the Italian, Austrian, and Russian ambassadors; events for the crowned prince of Liechtenstein and Karl von Hapsburg, the unofficial heir to the nonexistent Austrian throne; receptions and dinners for representatives for our sister states in China, India, and lower Austria; and a state dinner for the Oni of Ife, the spiritual leader of the Yorubas who had honored both Dick and me by initiating us as Yoruba chiefs on April 1, 1988. I treasure the beaded necklace given to me on that occasion. A deep blue circle with the white inscription "Chief Dagmar Celeste the Otunye Yeniwura of Ile Ife." That same year I also received a special gift from the Shawnee tribe as thanks for insisting that the Ohio Arts Council sponsor a special exhibit at the

Residence to showcase Native American contemporary artists. Like the African piece, it too had an almost identical blue beaded background with a white outline of Ohio and a red heart in the middle.

I vividly remember one evening when we entertained the Russian ambassador to the United States. We had spent the entire day in the first-ever state-sponsored National Conversion Conference, and by evening everyone was exhausted but elated. In his official toast, the ambassador related to us that this was the first time he had been invited to stay overnight in a private American home. He then told us how much he enjoyed and appreciated our warm hospitality in this most gracious private home. When it was the Dick's turn to reply, he carefully pointed out to this most distinguished and grateful guest that the Governor's Residence was not really representative of the average American home—nor was it typical public housing, though public housing it was.

Often the Governor's Residence is seen as an extension of the Governor and First Lady. But the fact of the matter is that this most public of all places takes much of its style and character from the whole administration and the many people who work together to create the right balance of official purpose and private comfort. While attention is focused on the First Family, it is those who make all of it come together who deserve our gratitude. Thanks to the extraordinary professionalism and nonpartisan attitude of the Residence staff team, the Residence was both a permanent showcase and a home for the First Family. Building that team and persuading our successors that it would be in their best interest to keep it in place was one of our most satisfying accomplishments.

It is an unofficial rule that the First Lady is in charge of the Mansion, or the Residence, as Dick insisted on calling it. But I refused to bear that responsibility alone. During our administration, a member of the governor's office staff was always accountable for the Residence. I contended that the official state residence required professional staff and that unless the Residence manager reported directly to someone on the governor's staff, she was not going to get the necessary respect. For without direct access to the governor and the Department of Administrative Services director, the Residence manager would simply be seen as the First Family's glorified housekeeper.

Finding the right manager was a big challenge. But when we finally did find Bobbie Wiard, we knew we'd found the best. She was exceptional, a professional to her fingertips, and she continued to serve the Voinoviches and Tafts discretely and loyally. Bobbie brought not only order and efficiency to the place but soul and serenity. Nonni Casino was the Residence chef throughout the first term, and her warmth and energy made the kitchen a favorite place for the whole family. When she left to start her own restaurant, we hired John Crawford, who came highly recommended but somehow never quite learned to love the challenges our kitchen and garden presented. After he left, we were lucky enough to find Frannie Packard. When she took over, we were all worn out from our attempt to hold things together on the social and personal fronts. I don't recall how Bobbie found her, but her competence was unmatched and her loyalty to the governor ran deep.

Running the Governor's Residence was a little bit like trying to run a conference center, catering service, and small hotel all at once. Even though I chose not to manage the place officially, I spent a fair amount of my time working directly with Bobbie to make sure that food, flowers, music, and all the rest of it were simple but outstanding. Fortunately, I had had my initiation in such matters many years before when I helped Chet and Steb set the appropriate tone and create the right atmosphere at Roosevelt House. Steb had created a wonderful team that made the social calendar of Roosevelt House not just busy but meaningful and interesting for all the guests and friends of the U.S. mission in India. From an open house for thousands every Christmas to intimate dinners with some of the most important people of the day and splendid evenings with the likes of Duke Ellington and Kirk Douglas, we somehow found a way to always do the best and remember that our mission was only as effective as the ambassador was loved and respected. For Indians, an invitation to Roosevelt House was a very special event, and I understood from the start that it was just as special for

Ohioans to be the guests of the governor, and that all members of the Residence team would need to ensure that all events were memorable.

The Residence was a workplace for quite a few state employees. The special unit of state troopers protecting the chief executive and the Residence, the house staff, and members of the First Lady unit all considered our home their office. In the beginning, that caused me and everyone else quite a bit of confusion. The phone system was the same throughout the house, and I heard it ring in my bedroom no matter whose extension was being called. Though we later modernized the equipment, the phone system remained probably the most annoying aspect of living there. Also, in the early days, Residence staff felt free to wander about the family spaces, including our private bedrooms, just because they were looking for me or one of the kids. Eventually we all agreed that our bedrooms were off limits, except to clean in the mornings. The offices for the Residence staff and for a portion of my staff were located on the refurbished third floor. I always insisted on having part of my staff in the governor's office in the Statehouse, because I felt that if all of us were isolated at the Residence, we would never be in the mainstream of events and could hardly know what was going on or have any influence on policies we cared about.

The thought of building a nest in the Mansion came to me that first winter in the Residence when I discovered an empty nest in the enormous tree spreading its elaborate branches at the center of the gardens. I realized that to those tiny winged creatures the tree must have seemed as overwhelming as that old house seemed to us. Still, they trusted that those many branches, while confusing like a maze, could also provide shelter and protection from sudden storms. The challenge was to pick the right spot and build the nest strong enough and with care. By the time I spotted it, the birds were long gone, the eggs laid and hatched, and the young dispatched on their independent flights. But the nest was still up there, a solid symbol of a job well done. My hope is that years from now we might remember how our family, while vulnerable, did survive the storms. How, despite the many disappointments, we grew wings sturdy enough to carry us beyond our wildest dreams. I am grateful for how, in the midst of the trials and tribulations of public life, we managed to build a nest strong enough to keep us safe and together throughout those years.

9

"I care enough to care about Ohio
So I am coming out to vote
for Dick Celeste"

We have to overcome evil in such a way
as to benefit the evil doer.
—*Edith Stein*

Lakewood, Ohio
November 23, 1995

Yesterday, while watching cartoons with my grandchildren Eleanor, Max, and Julia, I caught a glimpse of the cowardly lion still looking for courage and wondered whether I had sufficient courage to start all over again on my own. Building a new life alone seems daunting, especially when still haunted by anger and grief. I was curled up on the couch of the family room in Christopher and Melanie's new home in Columbus, and wave after wave of anxiety flooded my whole being. Have I completely lost heart?

The way I spoke to Noelle and Chris this evening was certainly less than loving. Of course, I want to believe that Christopher can do better with Melanie than I did with Dick, but I also resent the fact that he seemed to criticize Noelle for having lost hope in marriage for the time being. I simply wanted to encourage her to believe that she can find much happiness and contentment in other lifestyles of her own choosing. I want my daughters to be whole, healthy women before they embark on the mysterious challenge of a commitment to one person for better and for worse and for life. I want so much to help them avoid the pain I am suffering now. But in the dim light of dawn, I also felt very sorry that I showed no empathy for Christopher, who is struggling so valiantly to keep his own dream alive. I honestly regret that my doubts and despair appeared to devalue his certainty. Both he and Eric are good examples of men who honestly try to accept the sacrifices involved with marriage without losing their joy and freedom of heart. I honestly hope that they will reach and find rest in the beauty and solitude of their souls without ever abandoning the sacred love they share with their spouses.

147

As James Thurber said, "All of us should strive to learn before we die what we are running from, and to, and why." Maybe this Thanksgiving I can discover that much. Dick and I were certainly both running toward and away from each other without really understanding why. Neither of us was a true friend to our own selves; and without compassion for our own selves, we could not be true to each other. Then again, true love is less tested by duration than intensity. True friendship lives on and finds new ways to grow. By that measure we have been good enough companions. Nevertheless, both of our recoverings will require us to rediscover our very own particular Loving Presence and recover the relationship with our selves before we can imagine forgiving each other and all the rest who were intent on breaking us up. Perhaps someday I will have healed enough to trust Dick's latest promise, that beyond marriage and divorce we will grow in friendship and become the soul friends we were meant to be.

Maybe this Thanksgiving I will simply be grateful for the challenge of recovering together while apart and be hopeful that by Thanksgiving 2000 we will have shifted our relationship once again to become "for better" than "for worse." A lifelong friendship, like a long-lasting marriage, is not about intense passion and pain-filled connections; nor is it a conflict-free blending of enlightened minds. True friendships are more like ongoing conversations, dialogues that continue over a lifetime and beyond. True friends trust one another enough to let their guards down, let real feelings flow, and let go of all preconceived notions while following the voice of the Loving Presence often found in surprising places. I believe that kind of friendship will become possible only when I am ready to listen without judging and able to feel joy at simply knowing that my friend is well and sound somewhere out there in one and the same world. Such hope may then be reason enough to live and reason enough to move on beyond the angry anxiety of these cruel times.

Maybe this Thanksgiving I will simply accept that for the time being my truest friends are those around me in the here and now. This little band of lovers, friends, sons and daughters, and grandchildren are sufficient and provide enough family for now. Maybe this Thanksgiving I will let go of this unhealthy desire for perfection—no more yearning for loving accep-

tance from my father, for the dream of a happy family, for a faithful spouse. What I long to long for is to be strong again, to understand myself enough to be well enough to regain innocence and peace. I suppose I always knew that while no one can be completely self-sufficient, all of us are meant to be free. And now I see that old truth with new eyes. While I am grateful for friends, I have come to treasure freedom even more than friendship.

In remembering my childhood and youth, I choose to use those fragile fragments to help piece together a life worth living. Perhaps it is true that we can never go home again, but it is equally true that what we do somehow leads us toward home. I know I have all it takes to do what I must and sufficient time to fulfill my destiny. Only by freely choosing a life of my own and finally accepting the responsibility of multiplying my talents can I fully share in the happiness of my children's hopes-come-true as well as show true compassion for the pain of their dreams deferred.

This morning I am still far away from such simple serenity. Today, I still feel trapped in my sorrow and frozen in my pain. But just opening my mind to the possibility of scaling back my useless expectations creates free space in which to experience whatever life presents right now. And that is challenge enough. The conversation with Chris and Noelle forced me to see how far off the path I am, how cold and hard-hearted I can be even with someone I love so much. As I remember Christopher sharing his dream for a better marriage than ours, I remember my younger self dreaming that same dream. As I watch Noelle struggling with the complexity and perplexity of living on her own, my heart slowly warms and begins to ache with her. I see Eric and Mary holding high hopes for Alex so that he will grow up able in body and happy in spirit, and I realize that to be a mother is both to suffer and celebrate with your children. As I watch Melanie, harassed by worry about too much to do and too little money, I remember myself at her age, oblivious to my own pain. I, too, wanted to keep growing, not just help my children to grow. And, like Melanie and Mary, I, too, held fast to the dream of earning advanced degrees while creating a home that could be a sanctuary to a fledgling family. Slowly I am beginning to feel empathy for my former selves.

At least this Thanksgiving I am no longer blind to my blindness. I can *even see how a few years ago Dick and Stephen wanted so much to have a safe refuge from the storms of work and school and found so little comfort and warmth in me. I can see so many other friends who needed empathy and reassurance and found in me plenty of enthusiasm but so little warmth. Perhaps this awakening is the wisdom I prayed for. I thank God for all that comes to me this day without my effort. The sun rising now and always, the love surrounding me now and always, my health, my hope, and my willingness to mend my ways and broken wings. Perhaps joy can coexist with grief. Perhaps simple gratitude is the best remedy for self-pity and fear.*

This Thanksgiving was as good as it gets. Chris and Melanie went to great trouble to accommodate so much family. Their new home looked lovely (they even rented tables and chairs, since their new living and dining rooms are still empty), and the feast was marvelous. When Dick called sometime that afternoon to wish everyone happy Thanksgiving, and me a happy birthday, he sounded somewhat sad. I am sure he missed us almost as much as we missed him. Why is it that we are all still so sad? Is it because a family without a dad is a sad thing? Is it because we fear we might never be able to transform our broken marriage into a working friendship? Is it because, even if friends, we can never piece together the family we lost? Despite all we lost, I trust that someday we will emerge into a wider circle of this concentric energy and that then and there a Loving Presence will open us both to our new horizon. Rainer Maria Rilke once wrote, "Be patient toward all that is unsolved in your heart and try to love the questions themselves, then one day you will be strong enough to live into the answers." And so for now I am grateful I am able to love the question burning in my heart—"Then what?"

T he first party in our new home on Lake Avenue was what was to become our annual Fourth of July picnic. Since our house was across the street from what is now Edgewater State Park, we had front-row seats to Cleveland's grand fireworks. It seemed only natural to invite our friends and their families to gather and celebrate Independence Day together. Over the years those friends became the core of our political constituency and remained our most responsive supporters. But July 4, 1969, was the most memorable of them all. We had just begun to collect our respective children and bring them inside to eat when suddenly the sky darkened ominously and everything began to blow about. Some of our guests were still on the front porch and saw people running by shouting, "A tornado is on the way! It's just minutes away!"

Everyone had made it inside, thank God, and down into the basement. Only my mother and Sonja Unger's dad did not follow our instructions; they decided that they had spent more than their share of time underground during World War II and were not about to risk dying in the basement. Together we sat and prayed and waited for the storm to pass. We told stories, sang songs, and somehow, in trying to keep the young ones calm, felt less afraid ourselves. I had no idea what to expect. I had never experienced even a tornado warning, let alone the real thing. When it came, it sounded like a train was moving through the house. We could hear glass smashing and things crashing above and around us.

And then, as swiftly as the twister came, it was gone. There was dead silence. When we came upstairs, I was amazed to find that most of the food was still on the table. My mother and her new friend were in shock but sitting safely on the living room sofa, and the window right next to them was completely gone, frame and all. There was glass everywhere, but they seemed calm and peaceful; they had not only survived but were now in the position to tell us in detail what happened and how it felt to be inside a tornado.

Our Fourth of July group, like our future political constituency, was a most diverse one. Old and young, men and women, black and white, liberal and conservative, Democrats and Republicans, straight and gay, Christians, Jews, and nonbelievers. Such diversity was not much of a novelty on the East Side of Cleveland, where many of our friends had come from, but a bit more unusual in those days on the West Side.

By 1970, Dick was ready to test his political fortunes. We had spent the previous year traveling from Catholic high school to Catholic high school describing to students the importance of leaving the safe zone of their own environments to risk learning about other cultures from the inside out. These seminars were sponsored by the Maryknoll Fathers, who were looking for more effective ways to encourage young people to consider serving the Church all over the world. Dick repeatedly made the point that everyone has a unique call, every person can make a difference, and that "we can do together" anything we set our minds and hearts to—even making peace instead of war.

The kids were skeptical. "But Mr. Celeste," asked one straightforward youngster at the Saint Edward High School event, "haven't there always been wars?"

"Maybe," Dick replied. "That's even more reason not to waste any more time and start looking for alternative ways to resolve conflicts." He inevitably ended up telling one of his favorite stories: "Once long ago the Chinese emperor commanded his prime minister to plant trees along the hot and dusty road leading to the palace. When after a week the trees were still not planted he called the minister and demanded to find out why his order had not been implemented. 'Your majesty,' replied the stunned man, 'it will take a hundred years before those trees will provide shade. Why the hurry?' The emperor took a deep breath and then proclaimed in a firm voice, 'In that case, my good man, we have not a minute to waste!'"

"So why don't you run for office yourself?" another eager youngster shot back.

That evening, driving home, I repeated the young man's question to Dick, and to my surprise he simply said, "I think he was right, we don't have a minute to waste." We began by having long conversations with family and friends about which office might be the most appropriate to seek. Up to this point, I knew only about national and city politics; I had no idea what a state representative was. Dick, however, knew from the start that his heart was set on state office. His father would have preferred a run for a congressional seat, since that might have opened the way more quickly to national prominence, but Dick, an educator at heart, insisted that state government was where the decisions about education, health, commerce—all that truly matters—are made. Ambivalent about politics, I would have loved to have lived in Washington, because so many of my foreign service friends were there and would continue to return there for home leave. But Dick convinced me that Ohio was our home and that it was here where all our dreams would come true. He was almost true to his word.

In those days Dick did not even know how to declare his candidacy. He called a journalist friend, who explained what to do: "Just sit down and write a press release. Describe who you are and why you think you would be a good state representative." Dick did just that and then called back to read him his master essay. After a few minutes the man interrupted the lengthy flow and simply said: "Look, you need to learn right now to say what needs to be said in less than one page." It took much longer to edit the text than it had to write it. Still, Dick hand-delivered the release to the *Lakewood Sun Post* that very day. Our first race was on.

I began assembling a team of volunteers, starting with my baby-sitters. The Panehal girls were the first to sign up, and they then brought their friends from Saint Augustine Academy, who brought their friends from Saint Edward High School. Eventually, Peggy O'Riley brought kids from Lakewood High. Our Lakewood campaign headquarters became a youth center of sorts. Kids would come to do their homework and then go out to canvass. When they returned, we always had pop and doughnuts; after the hard work, we knew how to play and have lots of fun. They painted the walls with psychedelic landscapes and long hours. The front of the headquarters was creative but respectable. Will Trout, who had helped us remodel our home after the tornado, designed a bright-blue backdrop covered with stars; it said in large, lowercase letters "celeste." The true-blue and the stars were a starting point for our first and best bumper sticker, which I designed; it was a red-white-and-blue take-off on the very popular Peter Max graphics. Years later, for my thirtieth birthday, Dick surprised me with an original Peter Max bright-orange guardian angel with silver-gray wings. She is surrounded by sky-blue light and above her fly two large and two small doves. This celestial being stands in a prayerful posture contemplating our world.

The one desk in front of our campaign headquarters was staffed by a volunteer receptionist, and throughout most of the campaign many thought that was all we had—one desk and one volunteer staff person. (But on election night, when our opponents finally arrived to concede the race, they were stunned to find that when they turned the corner past the star-studded screen, there were hundreds of people and maps and charts everywhere. George Usher realized that what beat him that night was not just a good name but a whole new way of doing politics.) John Kealy, our "coach," as the kids called him, was the volunteer director, and Sharon Austin did most of the day-to-day office work. Jim and Dee Asbeck coordinated the campaign and Jerry Austin and Dennis Heffernan kept Dick working day in and out. I simply did what needed doing and kept the house and kids afloat. Innovation and enthusiasm were the name of the game, and Dick, the consummate *magister ludi*, was in his element at last.

On election day we had young people at all the polling places handing out literature. There were so many that the Republicans called out the truant officer. The kids were told to go to school, even though they all had written permission from their parents to work at the polls. As soon as Dick discovered what had happened, he called the superintendent and in no uncertain terms reminded him that we intended to win and that Lakewood schools could not afford to alienate their new state representative. Within an hour they were all back at their posts. What was most disconcerting to me was that many of the kids were wearing Little League shirts with our opponent's name on their back and Celeste stickers just slightly above their heart on the front. But before we could face off with the Lakewood Republicans, we had to first win our own Democratic primary. In that race Dick had to beat more than one entrenched Irish name. In retrospect, the primary was almost tougher than the general election. There were many Catholic Democrats who had not forgiven Frank Celeste for leaving the church and becoming a Methodist and also quite a few Democrats who thought that Mayor Celeste had not been partisan enough. Still, despite all the ups and downs, I never doubted that we would win.

In 1973, we had our first Willaloo gathering at Salt Fork State Park. When we began those personal-political retreats, Dick and I were just about the only ones with children. Natalie had been born just in time for our first campaign, and it seemed that each new campaign was accompanied by a pregnancy, and each pregnancy was preceded by a major remodeling project at 9407 Lake Avenue.

Expanding the house to accommodate our ever-growing family and circle of friends was a real challenge and a lot of fun. But it meant postponing my own personal and professional ambitions, and that was a secret struggle I learned to hide even from myself. For the longest time, I was not aware how resentful I was becoming. Furthermore, the more Dick advanced politically, the more he was surrounded by fawning females who often made a spectacle of themselves right in front of me. More and more I felt in the way and unappreciated. But I repressed those negative thoughts and consoled myself with the knowledge that all my work and personal sacrifice would one day bear fruit and that my husband's success was my reward. Even in my own home I had come to accept campaign chaos. No place was safe from staff and volunteers, and there was precious little time for me or the kids in Dick's new life. Only much later did I understand that despite all the excitement of victories and grand political schemes, I started then to personally lose ground day by day. The very thing I was trying to work for—a safer world for my family and all families—was sidelined and often intentionally undermined by men and, sadly, even more by women whose professional and personal self-interest captured more and more of my husband's imagination and time.

When I arrived in America, I was confident and strong. Despite a very critical father, I felt inferior to no one. Even in New Haven, despite all the hardships and detours, I was sure of my ability to become who I was meant to be. Best of all, I believed I was the key to my own and my family's happiness. But by 1972, life had become a merry-go-round, and I was not even riding on it. I felt trapped and vaguely discontented much of the time. There was never enough money, always too much work, and Dick showed less and less interest in me as a distinct person separate from the family. I began to wonder whether we would ever recapture our relationship beyond parenting kids and supporting common political causes. One day, my friend Carol Stringer handed me *The Feminine Mystique,* by Betty Friedan. "You have to read this," she proclaimed in her slightly agitated way, "and then let's talk." It took a few weeks before I found the time to read it, but when I did, something inside me clicked into place.

In a way, I had always had a preference for women. I preferred my mother to my father, female teachers to male teachers, female saints to male ones, and even Mary to Jesus. I preferred spending time with my women friends in high school and at Oxford, until I met Dick. I believed that women could do almost anything they chose to do. I continue to believe that, but I have also come to recognize how our every choice is tainted by a patriarchal worldview that undermines women's self-worth. Now, I was not tamely tucked away in a suburb; my husband's exciting career involved me intimately, and I chose to have six kids after considering and rejecting abortion as an option. (I conceived Noelle despite the Pill, Natalie despite an IUD, and Stephen despite a diaphragm.) Outwardly my life did not even remotely resemble Betty Friedan's, but I knew I was not living up to my full potential, and I had begun to suspect that even our best efforts in politics were going to benefit only a very slim number of well-prepared professional, mostly childless, women.

Sometime soon after my feminist awakening, I accepted that there were others who seemed better equipped to service Dick's every whim, including his sexual preferences. After his first few betrayals, something inside me shifted, and I was no longer willing to spend the rest of my time on earth flattering his ego. I was beginning to become aware of my own desires and preferences and was eager to share these new insights with like-minded companions. Little things brought about major changes. Friends had to start doing their own laundry if they were going to live with us in order to work with Dick. They were going to make their own beds, and, yes, they might even have to feed themselves at times, although I did continue to cook for everyone until I went back to school and work.

Whenever I found time to come up for air in those days, I could see that our marriage was in trouble. But I also trusted that nothing could destroy our dream and that all I could manage to do right then was stay the course. Judith Maloney, who then was still a Sister of Saint Joseph and the director of education at Saint Coleman's, our parish church, had become a friend and adviser. She suggested I contact the Christian Life Center, where a priest was leading Marriage Encounters. Our marriage benefited immensely from that charismatic movement. We participated in three different encounters, including one in 1987, the year we celebrated our twenty-fifth wedding anniversary. When, less than a decade later, Dick decided to leave, he claimed that our marriage had been over for many years and that back in 1962 we were too young to know what we were doing. When I reminded him that we chose to renew our vows at those retreats and twenty-five years later in Dürnstein, he simply shrugged his shoulders and, in a barely audible voice, said, "That may have been the closest I ever came to blasphemy." Why is it when lovers or spouses leave they have to convince themselves that the love they are moving toward is the only true love they ever knew? Perhaps transformation depends on letting go of the past, but letting go is not forgetting! Is it necessary to erase the true beauty and meaningful insights of our youth? Is it necessary to erase all memory of past dreams and loves in order to fully awaken to new ones? Perhaps becoming whole is a balancing act requiring subtle grace and nerves of steel, and both extremes—no past, only past— throw us off balance. The challenge is to find our true center. In polarity therapy, the most hermetical point is neither positive nor negative; both are required to get a charge, but true healing hides between those polarities in the stillness of the neutral point.

When we were "too young to know any better," we loved each

other very much. The romance of marriage and motherhood was intoxicating. Each birth was a miracle and proof of passion and enduring love. But I now realize that while watching babies being born brings a husband closer to his wife as a human being, it makes it harder for him to continue to see her as a playmate. We worked hard at making our love last. For years we would set aside one weekend a month to go to one of the many beautiful state parks to be with each other and to talk as honestly as either one of us knew how about ourselves and the future we envisioned together. Today I almost feel we tried too hard. Maybe if we had worked less at understanding each other and simply enjoyed the vast distances and differences between us, we could have kept the marriage more vibrant. Too much processing took the mystery right out of our love. I thought I could overcome Dick's infidelities and become not only forgiving of him but even compassionate of the women who got caught in our web. I thought he could learn to become honest with me and them and that there would be enough breathing space for true love to continue to grow in our lives. While that was not to be, I continue to trust in God's promise that love will find a way always. Looking at our children and grandchildren and the many people who were helped by our coming together, I am very grateful for that much.

In this time of transition, I have come to value companions most of all. The list is endless and precious. Most dependable of all, however, is Roberta Steinbacher, who came into my life like a surprise gift, shining through the thick fog of my denial like an unexpected ray of sun. I needed a friend badly—someone just for me, someone who loved the person, not the personality. We met in the early 1970s at a retreat for women given by Sister Margaret Traxler at the beginning of the second wave of feminism in Ohio. Margaret had by then created the Institute for Women Today, an independent university by women for women. She had brought together some extraordinary women from around the world to serve as her volunteer faculty, and together they traveled all over the country empowering women wherever they went. Roberta's training as a clinical psychologist and her experience in academe made her a great choice as a member of the institute's faculty. Beyond her intellectual credentials, Roberta also was a true soul sister to Margaret and any of us in need of a practical and spiritual boost. When I met her, she had already left the convent, after sharing over a decade of her life with the Ursuline nuns in Kansas, and now she was struggling to decide whether to even remain a Catholic laywoman. One of her best friends, also a former nun, had been denied a Catholic burial only because she worked in the same building where a pro-choice group had its office. After the many other paradoxical experiences with the Church, this one seemed to be the final straw for her.

In reflecting on that time, I am beginning to understand that no one else could have converted me so completely to the cause of liberating myself, other women, and the female spirit of God than this wonder-filled sister disguised as a skeptic-scientist. Without her gentle but persistent prodding, I could not have reclaimed my own power. Together we began the journey into WomenSpace and a whole new way of being. My love for all that is female—in energy, space, church, and mystery—comes from my love for her. For a short while, her company was a daily blessing, hard to live without.

What I loved most about our friendship then was that she discovered and treasured the little girl inside me and encouraged me to remember that life could be fun and enjoyed best with "sisters of the skillet," as she is fond of quoting her former Mother Superior. I also love Roberta for her passion for new things and for her basic faith in people, especially women. She not only was a major figure in creating Cleveland's WomenSpace and Ohio Women Inc., but she also was the driving force behind the creation of the College of Urban Affairs at Cleveland State University. Just as she encouraged me to go back to school and earn degrees, she encouraged thousands of others— many of whom now occupy some of the most pivotal positions in public and not-for-profit endeavors—to pay attention to the needs of the city and its citizens.

. . .

Dick and I had been involved in many local and national campaigns. We had participated in movements from civil rights to women's rights. We had struggled hard in the peace movements of our day and won modest victories along the way. I had worked with the farm workers, and we even had the honor of providing hospitality to César Chávez. I worked for better and integrated schools through PACE, and together we championed affordable housing for the poor through CRASH. I started food banks through WSEM and helped raise money for Biafra. But nothing we'd done compared to the hard work that went into that first statewide campaign for lieutenant governor. If in 1970 few people cared who their state representative was, even fewer knew what a lieutenant governor did, despite the fact that at that time the lieutenant governor was elected independent of the governor (just as the secretary of state, treasurer, auditor, and attorney general still are in Ohio).

Why Dick chose to run for lieutenant governor instead of secretary of state is still a mystery to me. In fact, at our Willaloo that summer before the primary, some suggested that moving on in state rather than national politics was a mistake for someone with Dick's national connections and international credentials (a mistake only if your plan was to become president of the United States). Repeatedly Dick explained that significant change, had to be grown bottom up, not trickle down. He insisted that building a "constituency for change with conscience" would require a willingness to work very hard and stay close to home. He believed deeply that building safer and sounder communities was mostly in the hands of state government. Education, jobs, human services, health in all its many forms, and even our personal security and the very safety of our streets and homes are dependent on the state's ability and willingness to provide adequate support. He persistently pointed out to folks all over Ohio that the local government provides police protection, recreation, and sanitation; the national government protects our territory and can set national long-term priorities; but only at the state level are we able to pragmatically apply partnerships intimate enough and leadership effective enough to serve the people's real needs. He never tired of teaching that "the best governor is one who can translate the many conflicting and often contradictory dreams and wishes of our people into a budget that funds and nurtures real programs for real people, within real time lines." More so than at any other level of our democracy, state government is the place where "real people" coming together in "real time" can make a "real difference." State government is a challenge as big and complex as that of most corporations. To manage so much with so little control over personnel (civil service) and capital resources (taxes) is tough enough; to do it swimming against the current of the then almost revolutionary fervor of conservative Reaganomics was harder yet.

When Governor Rhodes coined the slogan "profit is not a dirty word in Ohio," he forgot to mention that it is illegal for the State of Ohio to make a profit. The only way the state of Ohio can get money is by raising taxes, and the only thing we are permitted to do with taxes is spend them or save them. The difference between Republican and Democratic public managers is that Democrats are willing to both raise taxes and spend them, while Republicans usually are unwilling to tax while continuing to spend at more or less the same rate. When either have the money, we may spend it on better or worse programs, benefiting fewer or more people, but we are not allowed to invest tax monies in for-profit ventures that would benefit the State coffers. We can create the equivalent of a savings account by keeping a healthy rainy-day fund, but only after fully funding and balancing the budget. So, the bottom line for the public sector is how well we serve how many—not how many we make wealthy. The public sector is best equipped to protect life and liberty, while the preservation of healthy profit incentives is the private sector's challenge. To make money we need a healthy private sector; to spend it responsibly we need a democratically elected public sector to manage the redistribution of our wealth so that the pursuit of happiness becomes a real possibility for more people. The greatest political-economic challenge may well be not only how to continue to free the world for democracy but how to begin to liberate our democracy from excessive individualism and unbridled corporate greed.

"The personal is political" has been the most quoted principle of the feminist movement, and the political is never more personal than it is for those of us who in each generation put our lives, our fortunes, and our honor on the line and take the considerable personal-political risks of public life. In political campaigns, you lose control over all three of them. Your life might be taken; unexplained assassinations took the lives of some of the best in our generation. Politicians are not free to profit financially from their connections; in fact, financial gain beyond one's salary is highly suspect. (As governor, Dick was paid less than the director of the Columbus Zoo.) Furthermore, you cannot permit anyone you know or who cares about you to do business with the state or to collect a paycheck while working for you. Your kids can't work with you once you are elected, and we all know what happens to the wife. Much of what would be considered good, honorable, all-American, pro-family traits in folks who run a business for profit is labeled nepotism or cronyism in politics. And every year the rules are getting more and more confusing for friends and families and, especially, spouses. Then again, only in the United States do the spouses of city, state, and national leaders carry an honorary title of their own.

First Ladies—like Miss America, cheerleaders, and Magic Kingdoms—are a thoroughly American invention. Throughout American history, women, if not all First Ladies, have led the way in the struggle for civil and equal rights for all. Alexis de Tocqueville, an early visitor to this country and a keen observer, reported that one of the most extraordinary things about America was its women, and I believe that still holds true. In 1991–92, I taught a course at Kent State University entitled "From Leadership to Partnership: Emerging New Patterns in American Politics." The goal of the course was to show students that partnership, not patriarchy, is the wave of the future in personal, professional, and political relationships. I used the role of the First Lady in American politics as one of the symbols representing this fact. We read Riane Eisler's *The Chalice and the Blade*[1] and invited guest speakers from different walks of life to better make the point that, in this day and age, partnership process rather than dominator process is our best hope. Until quite recently, the mainstream of American women has always been much more progressive and independent than most women around the world, while American First Ladies have usually been more conservative than most American women. Furthermore, in contrast to many other countries, American women have tended to be more progressive than their men.

In the past, the husband was often viewed as a wimp if his wife seemed strong. We are now beginning to recognize that it takes a strong man to stand by his spouse and a good one to empower her. We also know from marriage as well as management literature that strong personal and professional partnerships are built on mutual respect and the ability to value diverse talents equally. Most people seem to finally begin to understand the distinction between power and influence. Using one's status as First Lady to spur discussion, foster consensus, help the partner reach a conclusion, and eventually sell the diverse stakeholders on the plan is quite different from exercising direct power or having the final say. Developing policy is not the same as deciding policy. Every cabinet member has more line power than the First Lady; but no other person in the administration is better equipped to bring diverse constituencies together to help forge a new consensus and develop appropriate, creative options for the president, governor, or mayor to pursue. Furthermore, no other member of the team has better access to the chief executive. The reality is that in most marriages spouses help each other whether they have official sanction to do so or not. I suspect that this is true around the world, but only in America are we beginning to accept the personal partner of a public person openly and honestly as an integral part of the official endeavor.

As women have become more visible, so wives have become more respected. That is the crux of the challenge now. If Bill and Hillary

1. Riane Eisler, *The Chalice and the Blade* (Harper and Row, 1987).

Clinton had been just friends or secret lovers, she not only could have helped him in any capacity he saw fit, but she could have been appropriately compensated for her work. This is why some politically ambitious, savvy women have at times preferred the role of the mistress to that of the spouse, thereby avoiding the taint of nepotism.

While around the world discrimination against wives is even more insidious and better hidden, that fact is small consolation to those of us here in the United States who have chosen to do our personal and political work in partnership with our spouses. Even within the feminist movement, the rights of the wife take a poor second to the rights of any other female. The feminist critique of the institution of marriage, while accurate, is insufficient, and we have yet to imagine beyond deconstruction how a feminist marriage could be different from a patriarchal one. Progressive First Ladies not only draw fire from the right wing politically but also disinterest from many of the feminist professionals in the media or even in their own husband's administration. Then again, who knows, maybe I'll live long enough to see a former First Lady become governor or senator or—dare I say it out loud—president.

The argument that political spouses should not be paid because their power is derivative is spurious, since others, such as consultants, schedulers, and press secretaries, are paid quite nicely, and their power is just as derivative. When a governor is a single male or female, people get hired to fulfill the official, ceremonial, and even substantive functions of the First Lady. But so long as wifely duties are defined by outmoded tradition, we will find excuses for exploiting sisters, wives, and First Ladies at home and at work. And since there is no agreed-upon job description for most of the roles women play, they can never succeed, or even feel like they have done well enough. A major problem with unwritten rules, traditions, and expectations is that they change at whim. Being First Lady is sometimes delightful but always dangerous. She is a bit like the queen in the game of chess. She has more mobility than the king or any of his men, so strategically she is the most important piece and should be protected at almost any cost. If the opponent captures her, the game is half-over. But she can be repaced by any pawn (all of which are female in chess) who manages to get across the battlefield. In politics, the adversary often understands this better than those closest to the office holder.

This queen analogy isn't too far-fetched. First Ladies, even more than their spouses, are even today obliged to carry much of the traditional expectation of royalty. They have to be, or at least appear to be, refined, in some unspecified, First Lady way. They have to appear to be untroubled and serene, kind and benevolent. They have to find the right balance between celebrity and concerned ordinary citizen. At a minimum they have to conform to the norms of the rich and famous of these United States. Their spouses, meanwhile, only have to act the part of a competent CEO with a dash of sex appeal thrown in for good measure and manliness. To make matters worse, the whole family, including pets, is considered public property. Yet there are moments of joy and purpose that make the commitment to public service seem almost sensible, and the role of the First Lady almost glamorous—in the best sense of the word—and sacrifices almost worthwhile.

In 1974 I had great hopes for myself and my family and great confidence in Richard F. Celeste and America. I knew little about Ohio, but I was young and strong and actually relished the thought of taking to the road in an RV and camping our way across this huge state. We never had much money, so dressing all the kids appropriately was a challenge. Early on in the campaign, we bought overalls for all of them at a small country store run by one of the many down-to-earth Democratic county chairmen we came to know and love. From then on they wore overalls to county fairs, overalls and striped t-shirts to political dinners, and just their underwear in the sweltering camper. The field of candidates in that lieutenant governor's race was crowded, and to win you had to learn to raise money, lots of money. I remember thinking to myself, "If it's true that we have to spend $150,000 to win, we are lost." Wrong on both counts. Ultimately, we spent only about $90,000 and we won that election anyway.

Still, $150,000 seemed like a fortune to me, not to mention the millions we had to raise both in 1978 and finally in 1982 to win the governor's race. On election night, after the votes were counted and we knew we had won the governorship, Dick and I celebrated with our family, volunteers, and supporters in both Cleveland and Columbus. I was exhausted and relieved and so very grateful when we stepped on that plane in Cleveland. As we flew into a full moon on our way to Columbus, I remember thinking that it was thoughtless of us to fly together. What if we crash? What about the kids? And then a feeling of certainty and safety came over me as I seemed to hear my late sister's voice gently humming her favorite tune, "Blue Moon." I relaxed and placed my head on Dick's shoulder, feeling happy and safe, if only for that night. I believed then that the best we could do for ourselves, our children, and even Ohio would be to love each other and let our love's overflow benefit us and them for many years to come.

That night I began to get a glimpse of how wide I would have to open my heart to include all those who wished to be a part of this adventure. I wondered also how I could remain true to my wild woman self so as to continue to include those on the outside of mainstream politics, especially my more radical feminist and lesbian sisters. Participation and cooperation were key concepts at the heart of Celestial politics. From the August primary and the heat of the battle in 1968 at that fateful Democratic Convention in Chicago to the Kent State shootings in the spring of 1970; from the innumerable voter registration drives, campaigns, and causes to participation in AlAnon, Part II, City Year, and Habitat for Humanity—during all those years, participation and cooperation were our key values and the best means, but not the only ends. Over time, that political philosophy became the foundation of my own expansive notions of partnership and peace, both personally and politically.

Little did I realize that my fear of crashing that night was also a friendly clue from the moon and beyond. If only I could have been wiser; if only I had taken time out then and there to listen more attentively. Instead, I plunged into a frantic, almost insane lifestyle. Looking back on that wonder-filled, victorious night, I realize that that was the first of too many times our kids would be left behind. Today I know that it would have been better had I focused more on our children and less on my spouse. It was Albert Einstein who said, "Mothers around the world must sow the seeds of peace in their children." Politically, I have done more than my fair share to unify Ohio for peace by opening doors to all those willing and able to work together. But at home I fell short. The stress of constant outside attacks made me oblivious to inside betrayals. Too often I missed the pain, heartaches, and confusion of our own children while binding the wounds of strangers. For that and so much more, I am truly sorry.

10

"Do you care enough to
care about Ohio?
Are you proud to say
Ohio is your home?"

At noontime
The cricket sets up
A high pitched
Singing in her wings
—*Sappho*

Vienna, Austria
December 31, 1995

On this last day of the year, I can't help but look back. I recall 1994 ending with a New Year's dinner for Mutti and the kids at Spagio's in Columbus. After that I went to LeeAnn Massucci's newly opened Clubhouse Café, staying just long enough for the midnight champagne toast. Then I drove home through what seemed an almost deserted Columbus downtown—crying so hard I could hardly see the road ahead of me. All I could think was how hard that Christmas season had been. Dick chose Christmas Eve—still a full six months before our divorce even became final—to become engaged. That diamond he placed on her finger as a symbol of his devotion will instead someday serve to remind her of his capacity for cruelty and callous disregard for even the simplest restraint.

Sitting here at home in Vienna, with the snow gently falling all around the illuminated outdoor pine tree, I can still taste the pain of last Christmas. But I also recall the beauty and peace of the most recent celebration. Mutti, the girls, and I decided to spend Christmas 1995 together in Vienna, and what a good idea it was. Following a simple but most moving Christmas Eve, we were invited to the American ambassador's residence for Christmas Day turkey and music.

Ambassador Swanee Hunt is a competent diplomat and talented composer and a most generous soul. She and her husband, Charles Arnsbacher, are down-to-earth, good people. Being in the ambassador's residence brought back memories of time spent with Milt and Roz Wolf in that same house. It also brought back memories of Christmases at Roosevelt House in New Delhi and the many Yuletide celebrations at the Governor's Residence in Ohio. At some point that day, Swanee asked everyone to share the happiest memory of the past year. Since I had broken my front tooth on a turkey bone just minutes before my turn, I simply said that, considering the past year, this very dinner might well become my best memory of 1995.

When we returned from the American embassy residence we called Stephen back home in the States. We could hear in his voice that he felt confused and lonely and was happy to hear from us; we comforted ourselves in the knowledge that he would be joining us in time for New Year's Eve. My thoughts of Stephen were especially strong that day. Early that morning at Mass, I noticed a young man about Stephen's age who was wearing, of all things, a Cleveland Indians jacket (mercifully without Wahoo) and a ski cap that shouted "Fuck parental advice." I laughed out loud. There are no coincidences! When I asked him whether he understood the meaning of the slogan, he just shrugged his shoulders and grinned. "Shades of Stephen," I thought and went on my way, smiling at the incongruity of such a Christmas morning encounter.

Then I decided to stop at the cemetery to wish Utzi and Vati a Merry Christmas. I also stopped at the Neuland women's gravesite to pay my respects and share my gratitude with those great teachers from my youth. At Vati's grave I recalled how Dick seemed to stand by me throughout Vati's funeral service and how all of us, including the local parish priest, were completely fooled. But the fact that he left less than twenty-four hours after the funeral could have been a clue. But instead I bought his explanation that Hillary Clinton's health initiative simply could not do without him and was grateful that he found time to attend Vati's funeral. I, who spent months sitting with my dying mother-in-law and helped care for her every day, was grateful for the twenty-four hours this very important man "sacrificed" to help his wife and mother-in-law through this sad passage. Standing at my father and sister's grave sites that snowy Christmas morning, I had to acknowledge that the man I lost to death had one important quality that put him head and shoulders above the man I lost to divorce: my father was a man of his word. He made few promises, but those he made he kept. He never told me he loved me, but he never deserted me either. In contrast, my husband made many promises to me and kept precious few. And while assuring me of his love almost every day, he never stopped deceiving me. But there in the quiet cemetery I decided it was time to let go, realizing that the energy it takes to keep myself miserable might be better spent to make myself strong. The time had come to transform my fear of loneliness into an appreciation of the value of solitude and freedom.

The challenge for me was to slowly accept the brutal truth that neither my father nor my husband were able to give me the love I deserved. Each in his own way was terribly cruel, and I loved them nevertheless. But they were also both perfect examples of courage under fire, and I am grateful to have had the privilege of apprenticing under such strategic masters. The fact is that they, too, had been wounded and raised to suffer in silence and solitude. Both would rather have died than accept their pain or make real amends. Or in Rilke's words, "Everything terrible is in its deepest being something helpless that pleads for help."

. . .

January 1, 1996
Peace Day and Kwanzaa
As usual, I awoke before sunrise—just as they were celebrating New Year's Eve at home. But where is home? Not with Dick in California; there is no space for me in his pursuit of a new wife and Hollywood-celebrity life. Not with Roberta in Maryland; she is well cared for by her friends there. Not with LeeAnn; her home is with Lori. Not with Eric and Mary in Boston or Christopher and Melanie in Ohio. Should I call anyone? Does it really matter? I am simply too worn out, even though wide awake, to look for numbers or search for words. Maybe they are all asleep anyway, or making love to inaugurate the New Year.

After that I could not sleep. I got out of bed and down on my knees and said the serenity prayer. I then fixed some coffee and sat down to read and meditate. It wasn't long before I heard the church bells pealing their New Year's morning greetings. At first they sounded far away. But then they seemed to come closer, until they melted into my heartbeat and for a brief moment their vibrations and mine were one.

Last night at midnight at the Heurigen, the sound of the Bummerin (the large bell symbolizing Austria's postwar rebirth) high above Vienna's Saint Stephen Cathedral was heard for the first time throughout the world. It was ringing in the year Vienna will celebrate her thousandth birthday. The bell's deep rings gave way to the sweet strains of the "Blue Danube Waltz," and I dissolved into soft sobbing.

What is it about Austria that she cannot forget her grandeur? How does Vienna continue to capture the imagination of this modern world? What is it about us Austrians that inspires us to ritualize, even sacramentalize, the most ordinary, everyday events? Are her saint and royal ancestor, still determined to bring the whole world together in one great sound harmony? Under Empress Maria Theresia, "Tu felix Austria nube" was the motto of the empire. Her notion of keeping the peace by intermarrying her children with potential contenders for her throne was inspired and exemplary female strategy. Perhaps the difference between male and female strategy is often that men envision empires lasting thousands of years, if not forever, and are willing to fight innumerable wars over the same territories, while women dream of a time when all living creatures can find their way home into the comfort and security of one great family and more often try to keep the peace at all costs. Maria Theresia came as close as any ruler in making such a dream come true. The difference between asserting that in the end we are all connected but alone and affirming that nothing can ever separate us from the source that created and continues to sustain all may be another way of perceiving the male versus female perspective.

I savored the quiet dawning of New Year's Day 1996 gratefully and in the company of my Loving Presence. Solitude at predawn time and early morning meditation continues not only to protect my sanity, but reliably nurture my soul. When I finished my reading, I set about getting ready for the New Year's concert. The "Tanz ins Neue Jahr" (Dance into the New Year), choreographed by Suzanne Kimbauer, was delightful and just what I needed. On the way home from the Volkstheater, Natalie and I broke into a waltz of our own. I am sure that those who saw us laughing and twirling

round and round in the Burggasse U-Bahn station must have assumed we
were still suffering the effects of too much champagne the night before.

That morning I came to realize I was getting better. I felt comforted by
the Loving Presence of all my avatars: first and foremost Jesus and Mary
but also Christ and Buddha, Kali and Krishna, Mira and Miriam, Gaia,
Brigit, Pelle, Sophia, Scholastica, Cleo, Isis and Osiris, Oshun and other
Orishas, Hermes and Hecate, Hera and Venus, and even Jupiter—God
the Father—seemed less imposing. My gratitude list is endless and full of
surprises. "Thank you Love for bringing so much together at the end of this
mysteriously dark and painful year," was all I could pray.

That evening it stopped snowing. We lit the candles on the Christmas
tree once more, and I could sense my Self moving into the center of one of
the many tiny flickering flames. There I was embraced by the light, and,
in the midst of this cold winter, memories of past summers and hopeful vi-
sions of future family gatherings kept my spirits warm.

Our last child, Stephen, was born on August 16, 1977. I had planned to be sterilized right after my thirty-fifth birthday, only to
discover a few weeks before my appointment that I was pregnant
again. Dick had started a statewide campaign for governor, so I resigned myself to another long, lonely, and strenuous pregnancy. Even
when I was much younger, I never much liked being pregnant; but
at almost thirty-six, I felt too worn out to do it again—almost.

I was working as a part-time conference director at the Academy
for Contemporary Problems (now the Mershon Center), a national
think tank in Columbus, serving the research needs of a variety of national associations of public officials. I shared an office with Marnie
Shaul who had just finished her doctorate in economics and had been
hired by the Academy to coordinate groundbreaking projects for the
Dayton-based Kettering Foundation. I assisted her with administrative chores, with managing and coordinating the many public policy
conferences the Academy sponsored. I enjoyed my work most of all

because it proved that I could support at least myself, if not all five kids, and that I could stand on my own two feet if something happened to Dick or our marriage.

Part of the benefits package at the Academy was a tuition waiver at Ohio State University. Up to then, I had only taken a few courses at Cuyahoga Community College, so I was now very eager to continue work toward my undergraduate degree. But in order to receive credit for my European education, I had to go from department chair to department chair, usually translate my records from the Austrian Department of Education for them, and describe the type of material I had to master back in my secondary school days. I could not simply take the equivalency examinations and demonstrate in English all I had learned in my youth. After months of running around, I accumulated about two years' worth of college credits and proceeded to enroll in German and English literature classes, which is how I came to know Helen Fehervary and Marlene Longenecker. I worked with Helen independently, reading all of Christa Wolf's work and getting into heated discussions about my belief that Wolf was a closet feminist. Helen became one of my most interesting and exasperating conversational partners, and our friendship has endured for decades.

Marlene was teaching a seminar on Virginia Woolf, and my honors counselor recommended I look into it. I am very glad I followed her suggestion because to this day I have not encountered a better teacher than my friend Marlene. She kept us reading, writing, thinking, arguing, and dreaming the stuff, and throughout it all she was generous in spirit, graceful in presentation, wise in substance—quite simply a joy to learn from. Since then we've been friends, estranged, and friends again. I discovered that while I could learn from her, she could not shed the professor role and learn with or from me. When she decided to leave OSU's women studies department to become my chief of staff, she initially became invaluable as my ghostwriter, and together we even had opportunities to edit the governor's state of the state and inaugural addresses.

So that spring of 1977, I was taking college classes, raising five kids, working at the Academy, gearing up for the 1978 governor's race, *and* pregnant. When I fainted at work one day, I should have taken it as a warning; instead, I redoubled my efforts and kept moving. And when labor began in earnest, we were completely unprepared.

This time I knew beyond fear and even beyond hope that, for better or worse, this was going to be my last baby. I was never going to come near an obstetrician again. We planned to have a tubal ligation right after the baby's birth. But the paperwork presented some confusion and considerable delay. And it wasn't until after all the papers were found and signed that I could finally begin to focus on my breathing and birthing. We were in a regular room, no bright lights; I had brought my own music, and we had a wonderful midwife. Still, all the commotion over the lost paperwork meant I had lost the rhythm of the contractions early on and never managed to catch up to them. Now they were coming fast and furious. It was my most difficult birth.

At long last Stephen emerged, ready to do battle from the start. He was big, noisy, and adorable, and I was relieved. I even thought I was happy again. I had so many contradictory and ambiguous feelings. I was happy, yet I felt too old to raise another child. Everyone just crooned, "You just wait, this one will bring you the most comfort and joy. He will keep you young." True, Stephen has kept me on my toes, but I don't know that I've gotten any younger.

I am beginning to see that, as he matures, Stephen may indeed have grown to be the most intriguing and bewildering of all our children. He is a highly gifted young man and, like so many gifted people, impatient, alert, and overly sensitive. He is very creative and might be happiest throwing pots. He writes well and at times displays the wisdom of an old soul. He was only four years old when Dick became governor; consequently, he spent his whole childhood in anything but normal surroundings. But without Stephen, that gigantic house could never have felt like home; he brought excitement and joy into our lives. And when Stephen and I were left to fend for ourselves during and after the divorce, I became even more aware of how special he is and how grateful I am for the gifts he shares with me and the world.

Nevertheless, why do most women feel obliged to describe every pregnancy as primarily a positive experience? After centuries of women having to risk their very lives in order to give birth, shouldn't we have a better understanding of the many dangers and paradoxes this experience brings? Asking for empathy for the ambiguous feelings I had about beginning to raise a sixth child at almost forty should not have been threatening to anyone. Not every pregnancy is a blessing; some can be quite depressing. Birthing is often quite a struggle for mother and child, and, as in any battle, the outcome is not always what we hoped for, and the stakes are nothing less than our very lives. Is it any wonder, then, that we sometimes succumb to battle fatigue? Only my mother received the news of another pregnancy without feigned enthusiasm. After a lengthy silence, she reassured me that she would understand if I chose to have an abortion. This coming from her almost felt like an absolution and went a long way toward removing any fear I might have had of eternal damnation should I choose that way out. So what kept me from terminating this or any of the other of our many unexpected pregnancies? Perhaps it was my innermost Being that encouraged me to remain true to the little girl who loved her dolls and dreamed of becoming the best possible Mutti. Or to that young virgin bride who wanted to make love wide open to the possibility of creating life. How could I then get angry with a Loving Presence that continued to call me to Life?

I am certain that everyone is called beyond co-creative passion into co-creative partnership. Women and men—straight, gay, bisexual, asexual, celibate, promiscuous, young and old, single, married, divorced—are called to love and commissioned together to create a Royal Realm right here and now. Procreation is not just about making babies; it is just as much about advocating for the whole of creation and moving toward a world safe for all babies. Take gay couples: many believe they should be denied access to the sacrament of marriage because their intercourse does not procreate. But what about their equally valuable co-creative possibility of working together to grow a stronger, healthier, and more compassionate community?

Often gay couples or single parents provide a calmer, more serene setting for children. The struggle to conceive a child, support it alone, or finally have the opportunity to adopt a child can be so difficult that once a gay couple finally gets a child, they often value that gift more than many who never had to fight for the simple privilege of becoming a parent, or retaining custody. Usually it matters little what our gender or color might be, whether the child is our own, our lover's, our friend's, or even a stranger's or enemy's.

To paraphrase Gertrude Stein, love is love is love. I would treasure a gay son-in-law or daughter-in-law just as much as a straight one. When Dick and I were married, my mother barely understood English. For years she called Dick her "son-in-love" until I finally explained to her that it might confuse folks. After a few minutes of reflection, she cheerfully proclaimed that she would continue to call him son-in-love because the law had nothing to do with her feelings for Dick. Following her lead, I believe we should rename "in-law" to "in-love" to emphasize the love that brings us together, not the law that often divides us. Maybe if we better understood the difference between law and love in and out of marriage, we would be better able to understand different kinds of partnerships. Then, instead of proclaiming our undying fidelity to a moribund institution, we could reclaim the power to grant each other forgiveness rather than divorces. And when a legal separation becomes unavoidable, we could part peacefully so that hopefully one day the relationships might transform and recover gracefully. Let us refrain from simply blaming those who break up rather than break down, and learn to respect rather than defame those who have opened love's space wide enough within marriage and other lifelong partnerships to free each other to become who we are called to be.

If trust is at the heart of love, and I think it is, then we should not be too surprised that many more women than ever before fall in love with each other. Unless they want a child or a father for their child, the battle of the sexes is hardly worth the energy. Between the feminist movement condoning lesbianism and state and church easing up on adultery, women's options have expanded while our trust in men has eroded. These days, marriages rarely last long enough to raise children fully, let alone provide emotional or financial security to women through their "golden years." Many women who never thought of sleeping with another woman but who no longer want to depend on men, either for procreation or for promotions, are deciding they would rather live alone and be free than live with someone who believes that, by virtue of matrimony, he holds exclusive rights to her body, mind, and soul while he continues to seduce or abuse any number of women, making a mockery of his marriage vows. More and more women resent and resist this double standard, but there are still way too many of us willing and ready to service sexists in the home, in politics, and in all the other professions.

Serial monogamy, while beneficial for upwardly mobile men and women, has been extremely damaging to their children. While life does go on, and families do transform and reconfigure and siblings can even grow closer through sharing pain and confusion, emotional security is severely shaken and trust in the sacredness of marriage is lost. Most painful of all, the belief in the magic and enchantment of a happy, healthy family is shattered, and the dream of the possibility of a lifelong covenant is at best severely battered and usually simply abandoned. The fact that more and more women have joined the exodus from the nuclear family and are opting for the now culturally dominant version of "the pursuit of happiness" only makes matters worse for more and more children.

But most harmful to spouses and children is when we mistakenly believe that only those people and things that serve us in subtle and not so subtle ways are worthy of love. This is when other addictions—sex, shopping, prescription drugs, alcohol, cigarettes—can become the natural consequence of an out-of-control ego. Then the explanation of "addiction" becomes an excuse that keeps self-will in the driver's seat. Recovering, while always possible, is unlikely for those with enough power to call the shots most of the time, and it has become almost impossible for the public to insist on a clear bill of health from addicted officials. We have to take them at their word and hope for the best. But recognizing addiction in one we love is difficult at best, and recognizing one's own addiction is almost impossible. I am deeply chagrined that, even as a trained addiction counselor, I completely missed the severity of my own love addiction. Shouldn't I have been able to at least recognize my own co-dependence and seen in Stephen's erratic acting out the symptoms of serious trouble on the home front? Even now the temptation to deny is often still intense. I had convinced myself that the marriage had to go on, and the price that the whole family eventually had to pay was unexpected and costly.

The wisest First Lady of them all, Eleanor Roosevelt, wrote, "We must face the unpalatable fact that we have, too often, a tendency to skim over; 'It wasn't my fault!' is an almost instinctive reaction to failure of any kind." And so I want to acknowledge for the record, right here and now, that the failure of our marriage was my fault too. I was unwilling to recognize the toxic nature of our relationship. I hope that by accepting my fair share of responsibility for that, I will be better able to recover and heal myself and my family.

· · ·

Where, after all, do universal human rights begin? In small places, close to home—so close and so small they cannot be seen on any maps of the world. Yet they are the world of the individual person: such are the places where every man, woman and child seeks equal justice, equal opportunity, equal dignity, without discrimination. Unless these rights have meaning there, they have little meaning anywhere. Without concerned citizen action to uphold them close to home, we shall look in vain for progress in the larger world.
—*Eleanor Roosevelt, in a speech to the United Nations, 1958*

I knew deep down that becoming First Lady, while hard work, was not seen by many as a "real" job anymore than keeping a home or raising six children had been. I also had honest doubts about my capabilities to hold the personal and political together in my own life; I would need to invent a way to liberate this First Lady to be more than just a wife. To complicate matters, I still felt like a bit of an outsider. Even simple matters like my accent sometimes became a campaign issue. Some considered it charming; most thought it irrelevant. But inevitably, if someone got into a heated political argument with me, they quickly became personal: "Where do you come from anyway—Ireland? New York?" God help me if they figured out that Austria was not Australia and that folks there did not even speak English!

Campaigning in some places was more like walking through a minefield. I knew that almost any move might cause an explosion. After awhile, though, I learned to stand up for what I believed despite the danger. Many people, including Dick, eventually came to admire, or at least respect, my courage. When people asked whether my outspokenness and spontaneity might be harmful to Dick's political aspiration, I would usually answer, "Well, maybe, but I have found that if people like what I have to say it helps Dick, and when they don't like what I do or say they feel sorry for him having to put up with me." It was meant as a joke, but it was in fact true enough. Today I realize that despite my bravado, over time I was experiencing a subtle but severe erosion of my self-worth. The media's persistent assumption back then was that a man who listened to his wife was not tough enough. And my feminist friends felt that settling for anything less than real line power was selling myself short. These opposing views pulled at me relentlessly.

By 1978, I had worked hard in many campaigns for others as well as in two state legislative campaigns and one statewide race of our own. The primary for Dick's state representative race had been vicious beyond belief. As I mentioned previously, racists spread rumors about me being black or Indian, hoping that such a charge would cost us votes. After all, Dick had spent four years in India and had brought back a foreign wife. To add fuel to the fire, that summer Tommy, a black child from Friendly Town, an inner-city exchange program, was living with us. Just like later on in our political career, when our support for gay rights meant to some that one or both of us must be gay, so our support for civil rights made us "nigger lovers," and one of us maybe even black. Fear of otherness is at the heart of real insanity, to be sure. Of course our opponents knew I was neither black nor Indian, but they fueled the rumor anyway. It did not work, however, mostly because both Dick and I walked the entire 49th District not once but twice in person, and enough people got to see me with their own eyes. As a World War II survivor, I had learned to resist propaganda by fighting back from the start. But most of Dick's political and media advisers thought differently. They imagined that if we ignored a bad story, it would go away more quickly. Perhaps both of us were right: it might go away more quickly, but the damage to our reputation and that of our friends would be permanent. Slowly they wore me down, and my fighting spirit started to diminish. I was defending on too many fronts, and little did I suspect that some of my worst detractors were sleeping with my husband.

And so the long, dark night of my soul began. It was on my return trip from Austria that fall when I had the first clue that something was shifting irrevocably inside me. Dick and I had taken Stephen to Vienna and left him with my mother while we went to Brussels to attend a conference organized by the European Community to honor outstanding U.S. legislators. In meeting after meeting with very high-placed European leaders, we were assured that environmentalists were just puppets of left-wing interest groups. I remember most clearly one exchange I had with members of the Montan Union (European Coal and Steel Union) who did not seem to understand that their own interests were not being served if Europe and the world went nuclear. After all, they were representing the coal and steel interests of their member nations, and the first people who would lose jobs were coal miners. But somehow their fear of environmentalists—the young and less powerful who chose to take their concerns to the street and then directly to the people by referendum—was deeper than their desire to look out for their own interests. After the meeting, Dick and I had a long and heated discussion. He was very sensible and pragmatic, as usual; he had liked our hosts and saw no reason to question their judgment. I, however, could not shake my strong intuition that these young European "green" activists were on to something and that our friends inside those international organizations were perched too high to even see the grassroots. I felt disconnected from Dick's seemingly more healthy pragmatism. I remember feeling at times as if I was standing outside of myself or hovering just slightly above my body and from there was watching us ever so slowly drift apart.

That could have been a clue. I now know that those sensations were the beginning signs of disassociating, but then I did not know how to name what I was experiencing. We went on to Rome, which was a first for me. Even though I had lived in Italy and speak Italian fluently, I had never been to the Eternal City, capital of Italy and seat of the Vatican. I remember standing in the Sistine Chapel and being flooded with indescribable foreboding. The altar paintings by Michelangelo depict heaven, purgatory, and hell. Hell, though, is the only part of the fresco at eye level when standing at the altar. Back in the days when priests celebrated Mass with their backs to the people, all those fortunate enough to celebrate with the Holy Father must have found themselves in hell. I tried hard to see heaven by bending far back and looking way up, but I could not endure that position very long. On the way out of the chapel, I turned back and noticed that as I stepped back from the altar, my horizon expanded, and I could finally catch a glimpse of Michelangelo's celestial vision.

Rome is stunning and very romantic. We stayed with Kathy and Jack Shirley, friends from our India days who were stationed at the American embasssy. Rome was their passion, and every day they introduced us to new sights, smells, and tastes. They lived a short walk away from a wonderful piazza with a large fountain at its center. In the evenings we would promenade around the monumental fountain, and then luxuriously linger in one of the many outdoor cafés, where we would usually close out the evening with a creamy cappuccino. One night we went to a cabaret built inside the ruins of old Rome. The players were sophisticated and very funny; the theme of the piece was intended as criticism directed at the smug, conventional heterosexuality of church and state in Italy. The audience was diverse and bizarre. That evening was the first time I experienced the glamour of drag queens expressed in an open cultural display.

It was in the middle of the performance when I felt the hot rush of my milk letting down. I also felt a deep contraction in my womb and a stabbing pain in my heart. I was missing my baby and my love. For a fleeting moment I felt both fully integrated in body, mind, and spirit and completely torn asunder. The milk was now soaking through my nursing pads and leaking down the sides of my body, and I knew I had to tear myself from the fun and find a private place to remove my dress and pump by hand the bounty going to waste in Rome while Stephen was missing it in Vienna. I did not feel guilty; it just made me sad that time and space made it impossible for me to be both the fun playmate spouse, enjoying the trip and an evening out with adults, and the good mother nursing her baby on demand. Most disconcerting, though, was this indescribable yearning to be free, to once again be open to a lover other than my spouse. I was torn in three different directions.

Throughout that trip I found new, surprising coincidences around every corner. The most ordinary objects became invested with the most extraordinary meanings. I remember wishing to be a painter, musician, magician, or poet so as to better hold on to this fleeting beauty and luminosity. Then euphoria abruptly turned to anxiety, and I began to fear that someone was stalking me. I never saw his face, but I could sense his presence and at times could feel his cool breath on the back of my neck.

By the time we returned to Vienna to pick up Stephen, my milk had almost dried up, and Stephen was unwilling to do his part to help it return. I still felt the rush whenever he would begin to whimper, but he had grown used to bottles and refused to work that hard for his supper. Dick went home early, but Stephen and I stayed for a while in order to visit with my parents and friends. On my transatlantic flight home, I read Ingeborg Bachmann's *Undine geht*. Suddenly I felt myself being pulled underwater by some mysterious current, yet I was still breathing air, fully aware of my surroundings, and perfectly capable of taking care of my baby, or so I thought. From then on clues of my impending breakdown were coming more frequently. Even when I was settled in at home again, I continued to have the unmistakable feeling that someone was stalking me.

And then I had a most unsettling phone conversation with Roberta that alerted her to my condition. I babbled and repeated phrases that made no sense: "Not to worry," I told her. "The little prince is here and everything is fine." When I hung up the phone and rushed to the baby's room to check on Stephen, I found him sound asleep and safe. I sat down across from his bassinet under a wind chime of little white ceramic doves. In my mind I could hear them chime like distant bells even though they simply hung there silently. And then the other mobile of five black seals dancing on colored balls hanging above the cradle began to swing wildly. While I was watching its antics over Stephen's head, it disappeared. A chill ran down my back. "What is going on here?" My throat was dry as desert air, and on my way to the kitchen to get a glass of water, I suddenly felt water oozing between the toes of my bare feet. The river seemed to rise up the hill, and I was terrified it would eventually swallow us up. I managed to drink the whole glass of water and calmed down a bit. I looked at my wristwatch. "Almost time for Dick to leave the office." "But he never leaves on time," some inner voice mocked. I was very afraid.

Time became the issue. "Too much time alone, not enough time with the kids, no time at all for anyone else." The thoughts were rushing at me and kept repeating themselves. I tore the watch from my wrist, carefully wrapping it in tissue paper to disguise it and to diminish the incessant ticking in my head. Then I threw it away. "Just in time, just before the explosion." The phone began to ring, and women friends from all over were calling to see if I was okay. As I found out later, just like Roberta, they too were confused and alarmed by my rambling and ranting.

Then my period came. I hardly made it to the bathroom before the clotted blood flushed out of me with the force of something pent up for far too long. And still I felt the water continue to rise under my feet. (In reality, the toilet was overflowing and the water had saturated the bathroom carpet.) I rushed back to the baby. He was still sound asleep. Thank God. Who knows what might have happened if he had started to scream. I remember believing he could only be safe if he was silent.

What happened next was horrible. Our dog Blacky, a gentle and affectionate creature, was standing outside the living room picture window, growling fiercely at something or someone inside with me. His teeth were bared and mouth was foaming. I was certain that if I let him inside he would tear me to pieces. I pulled the crucifix off the wall and proceeded toward him. He stopped the growling, sat down, and then stretched out and rolled over, whimpering softly. My use of the crucifix to calm the ranting and raging inside and around me was intuitive and came from a deep, subconscious certainty that I could trust Jesus to protect me from anything. I remember thinking that there was still plenty of health within me. But then terror struck again: I envisioned being inside the hell of the Sistine Chapel. Everything was alive and aflame, and I was inside this hell with no way out.

This is how Dick must have found me, standing straight and stiff, crucifix in hand, in the middle of the living room, stuck in hell. When I heard his calm, reassuring voice, fear for myself changed into fear for him. "I am ready to do anything, just spare his soul the tortures of this hell," was all I could think. Tears streamed down my cheeks, as if from some deep and secret well, and I found myself in his arms spontaneously confessing every secret I had ever held back. Perhaps I rested then; I don't remember. The next thing I do remember is sitting next to Dick with Stephen in my arms while we drove and drove and drove. It seemed forever. I was exhausted, convinced I was dying, feeling like life was slowly draining out of me along that road toward Cleveland. Dick had decided he could not handle this alone and was taking me to Roberta's house. He reasoned that as a trained clinical psychologist and a good friend who loved us both, she might find a way to stop my psychic disintegration.

When I arrived at her house in East Cleveland, I threw the baby at her and said, "Here, he's yours anyway." (Roberta is Stephen's godmother.) I truly believed she would be a better mother for him than I could ever be. Endless energy flew out of me. I could not stop talking, dancing, singing, rhyming. Worst of all, I could not sleep. Finally, Dick called my mother in Vienna for help. She came immediately and stayed with us, taking care of the kids, Dick, the house, and eventually me.

After a week or more of sleepless nights, Roberta decided to find help. She and Dick agreed it would be best to keep the story of my postpartum breakdown out of the press. She therefore had to be vague when asking others for advice, and the advice she got was equally vague. Dick, meanwhile, had left East Cleveland for the campaign trail. Since Roberta was not licensed to prescribe medication, and my hallucinations were not subsiding without it, it became clear to both Dick and her that I would need to be hospitalized. I was hardly enthusiastic about the prospect. On the way I tried to grab the steering wheel from Roberta and almost crashed us both into a telephone pole. The doctor at Mount Sinai Hospital in Cleveland tried to find the right kind of medication, but I did not respond well. Some drugs could not be used because of my past history of hepatitis, contracted from contaminated water while in India; others just did not seem to work. So he recommended electroshock therapy rather than continued experimentation with more medications. Thank God Dick refused his permission. Meanwhile, what little talk therapy I was receiving was not going well. I did not trust anyone—but then I was crazy. The doctor was the healthy one, yet he could hardly contain his anger when I insisted on maintaining some control over the discourse and the meaning of this experience.

I will be eternally grateful to Dick for listening to me despite my condition. I insisted I needed a different psychiatrist, preferably a woman, and Dick arranged for a transfer to Mount Carmel in Columbus. There I began to work with Dr. Rotraut Mosslehner, who not only was a woman but spoke German as well. This was quite significant, since my subconscious spoke only in German. After two months of hospitalization and more than six months of intensive drug and talk therapy, I began to improve.

With a good doctor, the support of family and friends, and less and less medication, I began to act more normal. I even returned to the campaign trail. But all of this had taken its toll on both Dick and me. While disappointed, neither of us was too surprised when we lost the 1978 governor's race. I came to realize that being sick is mostly a physical or psychological phenomenon, but getting better is a spiritual challenge as well. With the help of AA's twelve steps, I weaned myself from all the medication; and under the spiritual direction of Sister Francis Theresa Wojnicki, I continue my healing, day by day.

Decades in the harsh, critical limelight of Ohio politics and, most of all, Dick's request to accept his desire to be celibate throughout his second term eroded my fledgling self-confidence, even though at the time I thought we could both benefit from temporarily forgoing making love. I even thought celibacy might help us conserve and focus our energy on the tasks of serving Ohio as Governor and First Lady. Today I am amused and appalled at my naivete and feel abused and confused by my spouse's definition of celibacy. So I was grateful to Tom Crumm, who showed me and Stephen to ski the Aikido way, and to coaches Lee Ann Massucci and Mary Jo Ruggieri for reawakening my body and strengthening my sense of soul.

There was no doubt in the mind of anyone close to Dick that the narrow defeat for governor in 1978 had only whetted his appetite for a rematch. For a short while he considered going into business with his brother and father, but then he was appointed by President Jimmy Carter to take on the directorship of the U.S. Peace Corps. I never seriously considered accompanying him to Washington. We had a home in Cleveland I wanted to return to. Granted, it needed a lot of work, because Women Together, the first shelter for battered women in Ohio, had not maintained it well because of a lack of money and experience in those early days. But Cleveland was home, and Lake Avenue was the place where we could lick our wounds and regroup.

With six kids and very little money, a Washington move was not a realistic option. Anyway, as much as I loved that town—one of the most gracious cities in the world—I was not willing at that stage of our family's life to learn all over on whom to depend, what schools to send the kids to, where to shop for the freshest bread or get our car repaired, shirts laundered, and so on. I also wanted to stay close to my friends in WomenSpace. I wanted to get a job, go back to school, and empower myself. Furthermore, we believed that for Dick to stay viable politically and sustain the organization we had built so far, one of us had to continue to nurture that constituency "for change with conscience." Dick seemed grateful for my willingness to hold down the fort and leave him free to pursue yet another dream. Later, he helped me get appointed to the National Commission for Continuing Education so that we could have more time together in D.C. Since I also had decided to return to school, I truly cared about this issue and appreciated President Carter's confidence in me. "The toughest job you'll ever love" became my mantra, too.

Three years passed in a hurry, and in 1981 we decided to give our dream of winning the governorship another chance. One thing was certain: I could not campaign the same way I tried to in 1978. I had come to recognize my vulnerability and was ready this time to ask for help. I was not superwoman. I could not raise six kids, run a home, work at headquarters in Cleveland, hold down a job at WomenSpace, and hit the road in search of stray voters all on my own. Gayle Channing immediately volunteered to help staff my share of the campaign. This time the campaign director was willing to budget a modest amount for my campaign efforts. Roberta, of course, could be counted on, and many other women friends were eager to help me. Roberta suggested we hold a meeting at the home of Lesley B. Wells to help outline how to gather and focus all this female energy. Lesley did a wonderful job facilitating what was to be our first Core Circle meeting. I heard a lot of discussion about my shortcomings, balanced with enough positive affirmations of my strengths, to get me off to a flying start. At the end of that session we had made some practical decisions.

We considered not only issues I needed to raise, but constituencies we needed to help bring together. We decided to take responsibility for the smaller and medium-sized counties and to focus primarily on women. We resolved to compile information on those counties and discussed free media strategies at length, and we drew up a list of drivers and office volunteers for the daily paperwork mounting on my desk at the Cleveland campaign headquarters. To be honest, it was not all hard work; we had a lot of fun. All of us were excited by the prospect of victory and were beginning to understand the tremendous opportunities ahead for ourselves and women throughout Ohio. Much of my time on that campaign trail was spent with women friends, moving from county to county, radio station to radio station, exploring political and personal stories with folks from all walks of life. We filled in for RFC at party functions, fund-raisers, and wherever a group was too small, but still significant, for the candidate himself to attend. (Of course, Dick and I also made plenty of joint appearances. He was a great candidate—all the campaign had to do was to get him to an event and he would do the rest. His charisma was extraordinary; he could charm his way into the hearts of most. I knew even then that 90 percent of what we call charisma is really sex appeal, but I chose to trust him not to abuse his power or later his position.)

The most amazing transformation was in Etola Rowe, who in that campaign developed some honest passion for politics. Rowe and I had worked together for Gayle, and now all of us on Gayle's former Cuyahoga County Addiction Outreach Team had joined together for this political effort. We knew that this was a whole fresh opportunity to move beyond recovering one addict at a time. If we won, we would have a chance to streamline and consolidate departments and bring some sanity to the whole field of Ohio recovery services. I am proud that after all these years Rowe is still struggling inside state government and has been very instrumental in opening people's minds and hearts to the special needs of minority clients. Back then she often was the only black person in the room, especially in those small rural counties that seldom even had black residents of their own. There they still tended to call African Americans "Negroes" at best, and often worse. Some made some unbelievable comments to me as if my friend were invisible. Throughout it all, Rowe, notorious for her angry outbursts, not only kept her cool, but developed the zaniest sense of humor about the whole enterprise. I loved having her as my campaign companion because her tirades and jokes kept me honest and laughing.

All of us together organized a great campaign and when it was all over and victory was won, Ohio women—but especially me and my close companions—could honestly claim to have been "at the heart of it all." I believe we did so well together because we never lost sight of the power inherent in each and every one of us. No doubt history is served well, and politics is at its best, when together we raise the necessary energy to become all we are called to be.

11

"Do you believe we can do together
all the things we can't do alone?"

Life was meant to be lived,
and curiosity must be kept alive.
—*Eleanor Roosevelt*

Himmelblau, August 15, 1999
Feast of the Assumption

Once again I was up before dawn. Except this morning Noelle, Natalie, and Phina-Kai were awake and eager to watch the sunrise with me. They almost fell back asleep again just before the first sliver of the sun emerged from the water and transformed the crimson dawn into a bright, sunny morning, but a gentle nudge was enough to get them to at least open their eyes long enough to be a part of this ordinary island miracle. Phina was curled up against her mom, Noelle, and Sela, Natalie's dog, was snuggled tight against her. It seemed a reasonable assumption that all was well and safe for now.

I went inside to make some coffee and while waiting for it to brew found myself contemplating our collection of coffee mugs. The first one that caught my eye said: "Grandfather means more to those who love him than he could ever know." Dick came to mind first, but then in rapid succession Frank Celeste and Arthur Braun. Without their hard work and generosity, we could have never acquired Himmelblau. Marvin Robinson would not be an innkeeper today. I would not have a place to be with nature and all my family, and Bridie Blue Barn would not be home to TYRIAN. Without that equity, Christopher would not have been able to buy his second home, Natalie would not be able to be a full-time student again, and Noelle could not contemplate getting enough of a down payment to soon move herself and Phina into a home of their own. Next to the grandfather cup was a mug depicting a bunch of penguins making out, and a bright-blue mug proclaiming "Mary Boyle for United State Senate" sat next to a black and gold one with Mayor Michael R. White's signature promising "City of Cleveland at your service."

At this point I took all the mugs from the shelf and began to organize them in various ways. I lined up the half-dozen or so black and white Sacred Space mugs, reminding me that this year was Sacred Space's tenth anniversary and that together Kay, Cee Cee, Sarah, and I had sponsored more than two dozen healing retreats for women at Himmelblau. Next to them I placed a cobalt-blue cup that was a souvenir from Ruth Mary Power's visit to Villa Maria in Pennsylvania, the motherhouse of the Blue Nuns, more appropriately named Sisters of the Humility of Mary, the same order that founded Magnificat High School in Rocky River, Ohio, Gabriella's alma mater. "Fairfield Co. Courthouse," "Lancaster City Hall," "DGA—Democratic Governors Association—Planning for Victory"—all those mugs went into the political rather than the spiritual category. The "7th Anniversary—Amish Oak Furniture Co.—Loudonville, Ohio" mug brought back poignant memories of Dick's fiftieth birthday gift from the Celestial crowd; the desk, file cabinet, and matching oak bookshelves, now serving as the Himmelblau House B&B's kitchen office, were built by the Amish as a special gift to the sixty-fourth governor of Ohio. The "Three Rivers Pottery—Coshocton, Ohio," and "Warren Barr Pavilion Nursing Care Residence for Older Ohioans" cups are all mementos of past Capital for a Day visits. One of my favorite mugs features doves in flight and affirms, "United Way—Men and Women Working Together." Finally, the largest of them all, a gift from LeeAnn, depicts two crossed tennis rackets and heavenly blue forget-me-nots dancing around the rim. I found it interesting that this "mug meditation," this simple task of straightening and ordering, would bring me such a sense of calm and well-being.

Since it was the Feast of the Assumption, I decided to go to the 9:00 a.m. Mass at Saint Michael's. When I took my place a few rows back from the altar, I noticed that the Callahan family was assembled in the first row to celebrate Kathleen's First Communion. She looked beautiful and seemed quite shy. I so well remember that distant Holy Year of 1950, when I first stepped up to the altar to receive the body of Christ. The Feast of the Assumption Mass also always takes me back to Cleveland's Murray Hill and the fabulous food at Farmers' house, where we gathered with our Italian American supporters after the procession and mass at Holy Rosary; to Trieste and the May 15th celebrations at San Antonio; and to the Methodist Theological School of Ohio (Methesco), where in my final theology paper I tried valiantly to make the distinction between the mysterious phenomena of assumptions versus ascensions.

The first reading from Revelation 11:19 reminded me of singing in the Methesco gospel choir and Dick reading that very passage at Saint Peter in Chains in Cincinnati to accompany the first performance of the "Five Glorious Mysteries" composed by Rev. Todd O'Neill, Methesco's gospel choir director. The second reading, from 1 Corinthians 15:20–27, promising that "the last enemy to be destroyed by Christ is death," took me back in time to those student days in Delaware County when I first realized, to my complete surprise and astonishment, that we are meant to do even greater miracles than Jesus, including raising the dead. The only barrier to assuming our God-given power is lack of faith in ourselves and our God. The Gospel reading for that feast day was one of the most powerfully feminist passages in all of our sacred Christians texts. Luke 1:39–56 begins with a woman-to-woman encounter. Elizabeth greets Mary by blessing her womb, which in turn prompts the child in her own womb to leap for joy. It is this affirmation by her cousin that inspires Mary to accept and claim that blessing. The Magnificat, as her response, is one of the most radical passages in the New Testament. Her certainty that from "this day on all generations will call me blessed" is astonishing, and her faith in justice— "he has shown the strength of his arm and scattered the proud in their conceit," as well as "he has mercy on those who fear him . . . for he remembered his promise of mercy"—is extraordinary. This unmarried, pregnant, teenage girl gave birth to a "New Eve" in herself before she claimed the power to birth the "New Adam."

In his sermon, the priest reminded us how from the earliest apostolic times Christians believed in the Assumption. He told us that when Mary died surrounded by the apostles, Thomas, the doubting one, who was never where he was supposed to be, missed the entombment of the mother of Jesus. The apostles had already sealed the tomb because they feared that their enemies *might steal the body; but when Thomas appeared, he insisted on seeing the mother of his Lord one final time. So they took him to the tomb, broke open the seal, and, to their astonishment, found only fresh flowers in the tomb.*

Were the flowers blue roses? Earlier this year Mr. Seaholzer installed my gravestone in the Kelley's Island cemetery. I found the piece when my mother and I went looking for an appropriate statue of Mary to help us transform the stone pump house on the water's edge at Himmelblau into a simple grotto. The statue was named "Madonna of the Roses." When I tried to persuade Mutti to choose this authentic Arts and Crafts piece retrieved from on the grounds of a dismantled Chicago mansion, she resisted, exclaiming, "Oh no, she looks just like an ordinary woman, and sad enough to be a gravestone." Later that fall, when I returned to the nursery and saw that the Madonna of the Roses was still there, I decided to take Mutti's advice and invest in a tombstone for my final resting place. In the cemetery, I planted some Fourth of July roses next to her, and perhaps someday I will add a plaque with Teresa of Avila's motto, "Nade te Tube"—let nothing trouble you.

When Kathleen Callahan stepped up to receive Communion for the first time, she seemed both excited and serious. Behind her, the congregation gently began to sing the Communion hymn "Sing of Mary." When it was my turn to step up to the altar, we had reached the fourth verse of the song: "from the heart of blessed Mary, / from all saints the song ascends. / And the Church's strain reechoes / unto earth's remotest ends." After returning to my pew, I recalled the message given by Mary the day Gabriella and I visited Medjugorje. On May 25, 1989 (the feast of Corpus Christi), Mary in that day's appearance invited all her children to discover joy and love by opening themselves to God the way Nature opened herself to giving life and fruits. She ended that day's message with, "God doesn't want anything from you, only your surrender. . . . Pray to discover the greatness and Joy of life."

Ten years later, finding my life's joy is still a challenge. Audre Lord once wrote, "that deep and irreplaceable knowledge of my capacity for joy comes to demand from all my life that it be lived within the knowledge that such satisfaction is possible and does not have to be called marriage, nor god, nor an afterlife."

For today, however, it was sufficient to know that after church the girls and I would enjoy a leisurely breakfast and some good conversation, a gentle ferry crossing back to Cleveland, and a family cookout at the girls' house. Stephen, Dick, and Jacquelyn and their son, Sam, joined us for the cookout, and for a few hours, peaceful coexistence seemed possible (even though Dick was still visibly uncomfortable having both wives in the same place at the same time).

I left early to get to Rippepi's Funeral Home to pay my respects to the Zannoni family. Stella Zannoni, a longtime friend and supporter, had died the week before. Almost no sign of the suffering of the last month was traceable in Stella's face. She was draped in the shiny black cape of the Order of the Holy Sepulcher, with a bright-red Jerusalem cross pinned to her shoulder, and was decorated with numerous other signs of her past good works and importance. But what struck me most was that someone had placed a little amethyst stone under her rosary-draped hands. Paula, her daughter, told me that it was a good-bye gift from her grieving grandchildren. In many ancient traditions, amethysts represent the awakened third eye, and, of course, the color purple signifies wisdom. I was overwhelmed by the fragrance and sheer beauty of the massive flower offerings filling the room, and touched by the depth of the widower's sadness, which was matched only by his hope that somehow, somewhere, his love lives on and joy will return when, one fine day, they are reunited.

The end of this extraordinary day also has come to be the end of my story. Looking out across the dark lake toward the city's glittering skyline, I recall the African proverb that teaches "wisdom is knowing what to keep from the past." And I wonder when the power of the Yaruba initiation received in Ife, Nigeria, so many years ago would fully come into my life. Just recently Baba Ogunwande Adimbola—who was present with Dick and me at Ife and mysteriously came back into my life—told me that my title Iyalode Ottun Yeyeniwura means "Chief and Right Hand to Golden Mother," chief of all women of the tribe. Yeyeniwura, he thought, is also one of the Oni's many wives. The bracelet I received from the Oni connects me to Oshun (whose shrine at Osogbo in Nigeria is maintained by Susan Wanger, an Austrian artist who has lived there for more than forty years).

The overall message of the reading was to stay cool and tranquil, take re-sponsibility for the power given to me and, even though there is someone who is trying to lead me astray, rest assured that his plan will fail because I am a child of Oshun and well protected by her.

Deep down I felt in accord with his words. They reminded me of ad-vice given again and again by Francis Therese Wojnicki, my longtime spiritual director—to keep a free heart and be patient with all that is un-resolved in my heart. "Try to love the questions themselves," advises the poet Rainer Maria Rilke. "Do not seek the answers, which cannot be given because you would not be able to live them, and the point is to live every-thing. Live the questions now. Perhaps you will then gradually, without noticing it, live along some distant day into the answers."

After Helen Rhodes died, I asked her husband, former governor James Rhodes, if I could have some of her papers to add to Kent State University's Gubernatorial Spouse Collection. I was also curious to find out what role he thought she had played as First Lady of Ohio. To my great surprise, he said that, as far as he was concerned, she didn't play any kind of role. I was stunned, because I remembered her telling me that she stood for days on end in receiving lines and attended many events. Perhaps she was never interested or involved in public policy decision making, because as a family person she stayed pretty much in the background, especially during her hus-band's last term in office, but to say that her life had no historic sig-nificance was flat wrong.

It is true, though, that First Ladies can do as they please, provided they have the approval and consent of their spouses. First Lady Katie Gilligan made her contribution by volunteering in the mental health field, but she did not like politics. My successor, Janet Voinovich, who initially described herself as a family person and not too interested in doing hands-on public policy work, ended up contributing signifi-cantly to the well-being of children by expanding Children First, which reflected the Republican party's emphasis on family values. While Janet was a more traditional First Lady, Hope Taft promises to be another activist First Lady.

The informal rule is that First Ladies may have their own projects—especially if they deal with issues perceived to be feminine, like taking care of children, feeding the hungry, and visiting the sick—but they are not supposed to cross that invisible line and directly promote budgetary priorities. Nancy Reagan's involvement with addiction issues set the stage for extensive media coverage, and Barbara Bush followed suit with her work with literacy. However, when it became clear that Hillary Rodham Clinton's "little project"—national health care reform—represented the view of the president and intended to transform the whole economy of health care, the very fact that the First Lady was spearheading the health issue became its major problem.

Note another, more definite, informal rule: the wife must at least appear to take responsibility for the home and family. If something had gone wrong with our children, I would have been criticized much more severely than Dick, and even though I made a point of refusing to supervise the Governor's Residence staff, I still received criticism if something—anything, from flowers to food—was less than perfect.

I never perceived the role of the First Lady as one of power. Maybe that's to be attributed to my own, typically female lack of self-worth. Maybe I did have more power than I gave myself credit for, but I always looked at it in terms of having influence rather than power. Certainly, by virtue of being his spouse, I had the opportunity to become the governor's adviser. I did have frequent, if not regular, access to him and the people around him. Throughout all our campaigns, I was a valued adviser and active participant. I could choose to sit in on almost any meeting and attempt to persuade him and those around him to do things in ways that I felt were useful, particularly to women and the recovering populations. But ultimately I had no real vote and was expected to defend the official positions despite personal misgivings.

Sometimes I seemed to have too much influence and was seen as more powerful than I really was. As First Lady, I could usually count on getting a cabinet member on the phone, and anyone below the director would promptly return my calls. But then what? There were many people throughout the administration who, when asked to help, were only willing to do so because they feared to deny a request from the First Lady or the governor's office rather than because they agreed with us. Others may have been willing to help because there was a certain status attached to producing research and briefings or anything for use by the governor or me.

I believe I leveraged my position better than most First Ladies in Ohio's history because I benefited tremendously from the diverse experience and expertise of "femocrats" throughout state government, as did my staff. Thanks to them, my remarks were usually up to date and informative, and my assistance to those who asked for it was prompt and pragmatic. In retrospect, it perhaps seemed that I was doing more than I was and received more credit than I deserved. It is pretty easy to look effective and productive when one has thousands of people ready to help. I suppose that access to that much in-house support is a form of power that maybe does go beyond just influence.

I broke the mold on traditional First Ladies' projects when I focused my public policy efforts on women as individuals, not just on women as mothers or women as members of nuclear families. I set out to strengthen the status of women in Ohio, and I believed that one could do that by effecting public policy. Naturally, I began by seeking input from women.

In 1982, out of conversations held at Lesley B. Wells's home, the Core Circle was developed. This was a group of bright, energetic, and progressive women who helped me outline the best way to gather and focus female energy and to launch my efforts on behalf of the Celeste for Governor campaign. After Dick was elected, the Core Circle members became my permanent advisers in developing the role I would play as First Lady of Ohio. In addition to the Core Circle, there were other women and feminist leaders across the state who provided support as we set out to put Ohio women at the heart of it all. Four major areas of interest became my primary concerns during my time as First Lady: children and day care; the feminization of poverty and public policy; peace-making education, including dispute resolution and conflict management; and addiction recovery.

As a feminist, I believe that the personal is political; as a Democrat, I believe that government can play an effective role in our lives. When we combine these points of view, we come to realize that we make effective public policy when we base whatever we are trying to correct on our own experience and on the real experiences of those who ask for our help. Active listening is key in all good politics, and compassionate hearing is at the heart of all good government. For example, in raising six children I had experienced a great deal of what worked and what didn't work for mothers. (Remember, those were the days when day care was considered a socialist plot.) In order to be able to do more than just parent my children, I had to find ways of sharing that responsibility. One of the first organizations I joined was the Louisa May Alcott PTA. My friend Carol Stringer was the president, and, because there was so little participation on the part of parents, I became vice president at my second meeting. (That was quite a challenge, since in those days I didn't even know what Robert's Rules of Order were!) Carol's husband, Tony Stringer, was our councilman, and Carol was my first experience with the role of a political spouse. At home with five kids, Carol was the one who took constituency calls all day long while Tony was working as a lawyer or was downtown at city hall.

This was similar to the way my mother-in-law had functioned when Frank Celeste was mayor of Lakewood. And eventually this became my life, too. When Dick became a state representative, he was in Columbus most of the week while I was back in the district responding to the needs of our constituents. When I reached the point of wanting more out of life than just raising kids and answering the phone, I persuaded six female friends to share child care responsibilities; each of us took care of all the children one day a week, which left five days open for other interests. This is how I became involved in the PTA, the Cleveland League of Women Voters, and eventually the West Side Ecumenical Ministry, an interdenominational coalition of Christian churches. I also became the president of Biafran Relief and, together with Charles Van Winkle, then a brother of the Holy Cross order and a teacher at Saint Edward's, raised about $100,000 to build hospitals in Nigeria. I also served on the board of PACE, a citizen's group striving to reform public schools in the city of Cleveland, and when the Ursuline sisters started the Urban Community School, I became a volunteer. Throughout those years, I participated in local campaigns and spent my falls canvassing on foot and by phone. I helped Roberta Steinbacher and others create WomenSpace, returned to school, and eventually became director of the Women & Alcohol outreach program. None of that good work would have been possible had I not insisted on freeing up some time from mothering.

So I knew firsthand how important help with child care was for all women and their children. Furthermore, day care had become no longer just a women's issue. More and more men were beginning to experience the desire to find places for their children close to work in order to spend more time with them. By the time Eleanor, my first grandchild, was born, day care responsibilities had become a parental—not just maternal—challenge. My column "Daddy Needs Day Care Too" struck a responsive chord throughout Ohio. With the help of a very determined and focused staff, we set out to attempt to create day care for state employees. We began with children's issues because we thought they would be the easiest to tackle, and creating an on-site day care for our employees seemed a fairly simple first step. But we soon found that nothing in state government is that simple.

Finding space for the center became the first hurdle to overcome. We spoke to representatives of Trinity Cathedral Church, which is located across the street from the Statehouse. At first, they were willing, but then they backed out. President Reagan was threatening to take away tax privileges from churches that chose to provide day care beyond church-related activities. Next, we tried to negotiate with Nationwide Insurance, which had just completed building a new headquarters, and there was a possibility of usable space in their old facility. It looked promising for awhile, but eventually they told us that, on reflection, they felt that little kids running around their corporate lobby would tarnish their professional image.

Nine months later we were back looking for space in state government buildings. Bill Sykes, who was then the director of the Department of Administrative Services, finally found temporary space for Children First in a hearing room of the former Supreme Court building. Then the Ohio Historical Society stepped in and objected to us using that space because some valuable murals on the walls might be destroyed by sticky hands. We agreed to cover them up with Plexiglas, and Friedel Boehm, a local architect and fellow Austrian, designed and built the first center pro bono. Children First stayed there for a year on an experimental basis. Then, as the plans developed for a new state office tower, we lobbied for and captured more appropriate space and created a much larger center, which continues to serve children and their families to this day.

Prompted by Gayle Channing, my first chief of staff, Dick dedicated our first state fair to "Children at the Heart of It All." Gayle had high hopes of creating a full-fledged Department for Children's Services, but during our two terms in office there never seemed to be enough money or sufficient will to accomplish that. She also discovered fairly quickly that communication between different departments was rare, and the most needy children often fell through the cracks. When the First Lady's unit was asked to participate directly in developing the first strategic plan for human services, Gayle found a way to expand many a line item to increase services to kids. Together with many others of goodwill, we provided financial incentives to encourage coordinated case management for children and, most exiting of all, created the Children's Trust Fund. The unit's work on children's issues was so significant that the governor received a UNICEF award for improving the lives of Ohio's children more than any other U.S. governor.

My interest in peace education, dispute resolution, and conflict management stemmed from my very personal experience of living the first four years of my life in the middle of a war zone. I remember bombs falling, buildings blowing up, the rubble that was left behind, and the violence that came after the war when occupation forces commandeered our homes and raped our women. I suffered enough from warfare, and I didn't want our kids to grow up thinking that war was a viable way to resolve differences.

As a child and teenager in Austria, all the books I read, movies I saw, and history lessons I learned drilled into me the evils of warfare. But when I came to the United States, I was confronted with a very different mind-set. Americans saw war as a way of achieving status and glory. Until Vietnam, the United States had never lost a war, and the one attack on American territory at Pearl Harbor justified the dropping of two atomic bombs on civilian populations in retaliation for one attack on military ships and planes. The debate goes on over whether or not it was morally justifiable to drop an atomic bomb on Hiroshima in retaliation for what most of the world saw as a military skirmish at Pearl Harbor. Certainly the second attack on Nagasaki was inexcusable. We feel that as long as we can claim that we are only going after military targets, we are perfectly justified; however, in every modern war, all parties have targeted civilians, for terrorizing the innocent is an integral part of war, just as rape is an integral part of patriarchy.

The sad truth is that we become what we fight. In Bosnia, it appears to me that the same ethnic battles are still raging that inflamed the world during World War I. And while the Allied victory in World War II did not eliminate anti-Semitism, racism, or even fascism, it did facilitate a successful communist revolution. While wars may benefit some economies and arms dealers everywhere, war has seldom, if ever, empowered ordinary economic interests, let alone solved deep hatreds and complex problems.

As soon as Dick became governor, we created the Ohio Peacemaking Education Network (OPEN) and brought together the leadership of the many diverse peace groups in Ohio. We encouraged them to view our administration as a partner for peace together with any other group willing to join us. I hosted a retreat at Malabar Farm where together we developed an official mission statement and an action agenda. Throughout the eight years of the Celeste administration, OPEN held its annual meeting at the Residence. For nearly a decade, Ohio peace groups shared information, prepared a joint calendar, and planned fund-raisers together. Dick and I attended those events, encouraged friends to participate, supported the efforts of other peacemakers, and provided OPEN with space in a peace pavilion at the Ohio State Fair. During the International Year of Peace, Ohio received a United Nations award because of our extraordinary peacemaking education activities.

Furthermore, early in his first term as governor, Dick informed Al Dietzel, then the director of the Ohio Department of Development, that he wanted him to look at the issue of economic conversion. He felt that some of the smaller, war-dependent manufacturing industries in Ohio were very vulnerable in the event peace came to pass; and as governor, he wanted to find ways to help those companies transition from being completely dependent on defense contracts. Eventually, Ohio sponsored the first Economic Conversion Conference in the country spearheaded by a governor. More than two hundred Ohio businesses participated, and representatives from various branches of Ohio's state government discussed how they could assist Ohio's defense-dependent companies.

Another area where our peacemaking efforts bore fruit was the creation of the Ohio Commission on Dispute Resolution and Conflict Management. For the first time in U.S. history, all three branches of state government cooperated in the creation of such a commission. Supreme Court Justice Thomas Moyer, Speaker of the Ohio House Vernal Riffe, and Senate Leader Stanley Aronoff created the commission together with Governor Celeste and cooperatively appointed the first round of commissioners. Maybe one of my proudest achievements as First Lady was being sworn in as Speaker Riffe's appointment to that first commission. Thanks to the unflinching efforts of many, but especially Dennis Carey from the Kent State University

Peace Institute, and the many unpaid hours contributed by his wife, Marie, the Ohio Commission on Dispute Resolution and Conflict Management began to model the cooperative partnership it was created to teach. It is still doing extraordinary work in labor management cooperation within our judicial system, where procedures have been developed to reduce costly litigation. The commission is also helping Ohio's schools teach peaceful conflict resolution skills. Governor Voinovich initially tried to cut the funds for the commission, but he was quickly educated by lawyers, judges, and others on its merit.

But maybe the most important OPEN effort was the creation of the Holocaust Commission. When Dick became governor, Ohio did not yet have official commemorations of the Holocaust or for Martin Luther King Jr. This was brought to my attention by some OPEN members, and the rest is herstory. Dick asked me and Max Friedman to co-chair the Council on Holocaust Education and Herbert Hochhauser to direct it. Its most significant accomplishment was the creation of a curriculum to be taught in secondary schools on a voluntary basis. "Prejudice Unleashed" was such a well-designed curriculum, thanks to Leatrice Rabinsky and Carol Danks, that it became a model for teaching the Holocaust experience in Germany. Chairing that commission was a most solemn experience for me. The diversity of the members was astounding. Retired U.S. Army colonel Richard R. Seibel, the man who liberated the concentration camp closest to my hometown, happened to be from Defiance and was available to serve on the commission; so was one of the Mengele twins, and her testimony about helplessly watching Dr. Josef Mengele torture her twin sister to death moved all of us deeply. We also included representatives of the Ohio German community, especially representatives from the Greater Cleveland area, who were doubtful about the usefulness of studying the Holocaust. Because they feared being blamed collectively, they were reticent about signing the final report.

"Prejudice Unleashed" taught schoolchildren, through the Holocaust experience, how dangerous it is to discriminate and how quickly prejudice can turn into persecution. In some ways it was a course in anti-discrimination, allowing children to learn the dangers of discriminating against anyone who is different, whether by religion, race, gender, or sexual preference. But since the Jewish community was very adamant that the Holocaust experience not be diluted by all of the other possible discriminations that have occurred throughout human history before or since the Holocaust, we did downplay those other connections. It is my fervent hope that all churches, if not all schools, will continue this work. I do not anticipate a diminishing need for teaching respect for human rights.

I also became passionately involved in the reform of Ohio's mental health system. Having recovered from postpartum depression, I had some personal experience of mental *dis*-ease, and as the chair of the planning committee of the Cuyahoga County Mental Health Board, I had some professional experience as well. Furthermore, by the time Dick became governor, I had already worked in the alcohol and drug abuse field for almost four years and knew firsthand what worked and what didn't work with that population as well. Everyone in the field seemed to agree that there were too many different departments involved in delivering counseling services, especially as they related to addictions. Local agencies were burdened with too many reporting requirements to too many monitors within state government. A more focused service delivery system with a clearer emphasis on underserved populations such as minorities, women, the old, the young, homosexuals, and, especially, the disabled—was in demand.

Within the first six months of taking office, Dick appointed me to chair the Recovery Council, which then became the Recovery Commission. We held hearings in all major metropolitan areas throughout Ohio, and I listened to hundreds of hours of testimony and appointed committees to work with the council; eventually more than eighty recommendations were sent to the governor. The top recommendation was the creation of a cabinet-level Department of Recovery Services to consolidate alcohol and other drug addiction services as well as to explore the ever-expanding newer addictions, such as gambling, food, and sex. Even though we proved the need, a department could not be created immediately because the money was not available in that first budget. However, in the second term, with the help of Senator Grace Drake and Representative Ray Miller, we finally did manage to implement the Recovery Council's original recommendation to create a separate Department of Recovery Services. I wanted that particular name because it focused attention on the solution rather than the problem and would also include additional addiction problems, such as gambling, food, rage, and violence. The Republicans, however, were unwilling to do approve a more inclusive definition of "addiction." So we compromised and named the new department Ohio Department of Alcohol and Drug Addiction Services (ODADAS).

Some of the less controversial and less expensive Recovery Council recommendations immediately became priorities in the first Celeste administration. For example, the Liquor Department was given a mandate to sell less liquor but still make more money, which they did very effectively for eight years. They also started handing out literature about the dangers of abuse and alcoholism, and overnight Ohio liquor stores became touch points for recovery.

Another positive result of the work of the Recovery Council was the creation of the first Employee Assistance Program (EAP) for state employees. Ohio was the first state in the union to do so. We encouraged troubled employees to avail themselves of the program, working with the state employees' unions to change the rules so that supervisors could insist that their employees go to EAP. The First Lady's unit developed a training program, and I led the training team. We held training sessions in every department, beginning with the directors and deputy directors. Each cabinet member was then responsible for educating their respective staffs and department employees. It was the first time that the governor mandated that cabinet members show up for an addiction recovery in-service seminar. It was a challenge to get some directors to pay attention to this issue, and I know that many of them felt I was on a crusade—and maybe I was—but I also know that the Employee Assistance Program has made a difference in many people's lives. I've received hundreds of letters from family members thanking us for giving their loved ones the opportunity to take care of their addiction problem without the threat of job loss.

Getting the Health Department and the Mental Health Department to cooperate was not easy. The Mental Health Department had been responsible for dispersing drug-related monies, and the Health Department was responsible for alcohol-related funds. The alcoholics didn't want anything to do with the Mental Health Department, and no one wanted to have anything to do with the alcoholics. It was a bloody battle, and it took years to come up with a workable compromise. In the beginning I chaired the second Recovery Council, too, but eventually left because I could see the handwriting on the wall. There was not much hope of creating an independent department until much later, and I wanted to focus on other things. Pam Hyde, our director of mental health, persisted and helped create a local option process, which I think almost intensified the problem. Now each county had a choice of retaining their alcoholism council or folding it into the county mental health board, while originally, the idea was to combine services in either the Health or Mental Health Department. Folks would not acquiesce; and even after the creation of the Department of Alcohol and Drug Addiction Services, the problem of the monies flowing into the Health or Mental Health Department from the federal level lingered on.

Back then we did not think about sex addiction and what co-dependence to a sex addict looked or felt like. I am amazed at how cunning this disease is. Although I spent years working on recovery issues, had spent more than a decade in AlAnon, and even received my master's degree in addiction counseling from the Methodist Theological School, I never recognized my own co-dependence until after our divorce almost a decade later, when I finally got treatment for love addicition at the Meadows in Arizona. My denial was so corrosive that it almost destroyed me and eventually helped fragment the family I had spent my life building.

Another set of issues I chose to work on were those related to the feminization of poverty. We decided that for a policy to benefit everyone, it would have to benefit poverty-stricken women first. "Feminization of poverty" had become a catchphrase for the notion that by the year 2000, unless things changed drastically, almost 100 percent of the poverty class in America would be women and their children.

Since there was not much we could do about the rest of the nation, we in Ohio began to focus resources on women and children. Gayle Channing and others examined public policies, beginning with the Welfare Department, the Health Department, and Recovery Services. Such focus of state government services on women not only improved equality but also improved efficiency. In order to transform economic reality for families in Ohio, we believed we had to help women first. If we did not help women, the lives of their children could not be improved either. Even if both parents are together, which is only true in about 50 percent of the cases, both parents must work in order to make ends meet. Whenever my staff or I reviewed the general budget or any other program or proposal we supported or funded, we examined how it affected women. Others were interested in how our public policy impacted our people, but only the First Lady's unit took an interest in poverty-stricken women and whether whatever we were doing was helpful to them. And while we could not always bring about a complete change of priority, we did persuade many to raise new questions and made significant strides.

I encouraged Gayle to switch her focus from looking just at children to questioning how what we did affected their mothers, grandmothers, and other mostly female caretakers. Our unit monitored the various budgets in terms of how our services were affecting poverty-stricken, black, young, and older women. I had come to believe that any program that would benefit the most vulnerable women would in fact help all women, and what benefited women would favor the well-being of families and, thus, all of us. When we top-down design programs to help everyone, the benefits seldom, if ever, trickle down to those folks most in need.

State Senator Linda Furney of Toledo also put together a women's coalition to monitor the state budget from the legislative side.
By then Gayle had moved out of state government to create her own
consulting company, and I had hired Marlene Longenecker as my
chief of staff. Marlene was very instrumental in creating the Women's
Interagency Task Force. We recommended to the governor that he
require each cabinet member to select a competent feminist budget
policy adviser to represent their respective departments and then be
appointed to the newly created Women's Interagency Task Force. In
this way, each of the council members not only had the governor's
blessing but also the full support of their respective cabinet director
and access to the latest and most significant budget data. To this day,
many of these former task force members still network informally, but
effectively, within state government and across legislative partisan
boundaries.

Another area I took a personal interest in was women in prison.
Sister Margaret Traxler brought the plight of imprisoned women to
my attention. As I began my visits to Marysville Correctional Institution in 1983, I noticed that the treatment of women in prison, especially those on death row, was far worse than that of men. Furthermore, during conversations with these women, I came to realize that
many were in prison for retaliating against abusive partners. This was
not my first encounter with the battered women syndrome. In the
early seventies, WomenSpace hosted hearings at Cleveland State University that focused on the issue of domestic violence. Our focus was
exclusively on the victims of abuse rather than on creating treatment
opportunities for the abusers. At the end of that first hearing, a young
black man stood up and tried to tell us that whenever he was in an
intimate relationship, he found himself eventually provoked to violence. With tears in his eyes, he pleaded with us to help him curb his
violent behavior. None of us knew what to do. These were the early
seventies, and we had just barely opened Women Together, the first
shelter in Ohio for abused women and their children. (In fact, the first
battered women's shelter in the state of Ohio was our Cleveland home

on Lake Avenue.) We began to serve the needs of battered women, but they had barely developed treatment protocols for victims and could not begin to worry about the abusers, too. Jane Mazzarella, a wonderful addiction counselor, was the only person who tried, just before she died, to get funding for a program to treat alcoholic abusers for their additional addiction to rage and violence. After she died, it was more than a decade before Templum House in Cleveland picked up her banner in the late 1990s.

One of my most poignant memories as First Lady was my participation in the baptism of a woman on death row. A Baptist, she believed in full-submersion baptism, but the prison rules would not allow this. After her minister contacted me and I intervened with the prison authorities on her behalf, she was allowed to be submerged in a bathtub at the prison. She invited me to the event, and, though heavily guarded, I was permitted to attend. The whole experience reinforced how we dehumanize people once we imprison them. Her shackles were removed only briefly while submerged in the bathtub, and instead of assigning female guards to the event, male guards were permitted to watch. When she reemerged from the water, her face was truly transformed, but the thin white cotton gown had become almost transparent and was clinging to her body. The male guards laughed and jeered and ordered her to lean over a chair so they would not have to bend down to reapply the shackles to her feet. To this day, the blood rushes to my head whenever I think of that baptism, and I still feel her humiliation as my own.

After that experience, I was determined to find a way to improve the lives of women at Marysville. With the help of Ruth Mary Power HM, who by then had joined the First Lady unit staff, we increased spiritual counseling opportunities for the women and began to promote interest in creating an addiction recovery program, which has blossomed into the Tapestry Program. We also stepped up the research done on all women on death row and all battered women at Marysville. To do that, I had to become personally involved, not just politically concerned.

Very early in the first Celeste administration, Dick felt that government had become too removed, even distant, from the people. To remedy the situation somewhat, he decided to move the state capital from community to community, dubbing it "Capital for a Day." The whole bureaucracy was not moved, of course, but at least the cabinet, the governor's office, and key personnel throughout the administration spent a whole day and night in a number of communities around Ohio. We decided that the impact of such a gesture in the larger cities would be minimal; but in medium-sized towns people would be excited to be offered an opportunity to meet with their governor and the rest of those committed to serve them.

For me and my staff, it became quite a challenge to explore how to best schedule my time at those special events. Since I had shown great interest and enthusiasm for day care, I often was invited to visit a local day care facility or to sit down with groups planning to create a day care. Also, because of my professional expertise in the area of addiction recovery, I made a point of visiting treatment centers, halfway homes, and any other group struggling with the problems of addiction.

Gayle Channing had worked hard to manifest the governor's order to create ways for intercabinet and interagency cooperation. Early in the first term, we convened the first children's cluster meetings, which brought together all state departments that had responsibility for meeting children's needs. We encouraged them to sit around the same table and work out better ways of coordinating services. But helping folks cooperate at the top in Columbus was only the first step toward assuring that fewer kids fell between the cracks of the various child service bureaucracies. We assumed that the sooner we could encourage social workers, teachers, public health professionals, and other service providers to get together locally, the more effective the state cluster case management work would become. So we used Capital for a Day to make it happen in community after community. We invited all sorts of human service providers to share a brown bag lunch with me in order to empower folks from the bottom up to help us improve services to women and their children. Increasing participation was one of the key ingredients of Celestial politics, and it worked miracles on this issue, too.

A particularly fun inclusive event on our Capital for a Day visits was a twist on the idea of a First Lady's tea. I invited women leaders from all walks of life to join me for an afternoon tea (or sometimes it was lunch or coffee and dessert). An initial guest list was drawn up with the help of the local mayor's spouse, if there was one, and elected women officials, if there were any. We were also sure to include feminists and representatives of feminist groups, as well as directors of significant human service agencies and other institutions. We usually could count on the cooperation of the local chamber of commerce to share with us the names of women who owned or operated businesses. This was a significant group indeed, since small businesses were creating more jobs than all the Fortune 500 companies combined. Finally, we included spouses of community leaders and members of traditional women professions and topped off the networking with artists and electronic media representatives and female church leaders.

After everyone had a chance to sign in and get some refreshments, I began the program with a wonderful film entitled *One Fine Day,* which is a brief but inspiring rendition of the story of women through the course of history. It was the perfect way to get women in the mood to meet the women leaders of the Celeste cabinet. (Dick had appointed more women to cabinet positions than all the other governors throughout Ohio's history combined.) I would introduce them one by one and let them tell their own stories. Some were single, most were married; some had children, most did not. Some were black, some were gay; some had advanced degrees in their respective fields, some had hands-on experience; some had both. They talked about their childhood, whether they were most influenced by mothers or fathers, whether they had been good at sports, what it was like to be part of an ethnic or racial minority. Their sense of fun and excitement was contagious. They made everyone feel that we were in this together and that together we can do all the things we can't do alone. At the first few Capital for a Day presentations, some of the cabinet women were a bit shy and somewhat confused about the purpose of such role modeling. But over the years, they came to understand and appreciate how important, and even inspiring, it was for other women to hear intelligent, straightforward answers from women just like themselves who treated them like peers. Good politics is always about building strong constituencies from the ground up. Capital for a Day did all of that and more. Whenever we returned to Columbus, I was confident we left behind a more empowered community of women.

I even tried to bring together women across party lines. I attempted to network professional women with homemakers and spouses of political leaders, industrialists and professionals with academics and entrepreneurs, and always encouraged women to take back their own power. Furthermore, I was convinced that together we women could bring about change from the bottom up and become an integral part of the decision-making process in our communities. I believed then, and still do now, that together we can become powerful enough to have our voices not only heard but heeded. The women we brought to Columbus were feminists with clear-eyed vision and pragmatic ideas on how to change state government and open doors and create opportunities for all women.

Over time, it became clear that the First Lady's unit was a place where female state employees could register their complaints about discrimination and sexual harassment. Sexist behavior, when brought to my attention, was not tolerated. Today we are much more aware of how sexism manifests itself in the workplace and have created personal and professional guidelines and rules to prevent it, but at that time almost nowhere in state government were policies in place regarding harassment, let alone outright discrimination. Nevertheless, there were quite a few incidents, even in the governor's office, that went unpunished; and because it was such a closeted issue, those harassed had a hard time discussing it with their superiors, let alone become willing to take the harassers to court. More than a third of the people who wrote to me were state employees, so I decided to visit the different departments and have brown bag lunches with whoever chose to come. Many joined us and discussed issues such as day care, family-friendly employment policies, equal pay, and flextime. Nothing that affected female state employees was off-limits. The women were initially uncertain and close-mouthed but eventually opened up. Once I was in the room and they realized I was there to listen, their discomfort and fear melted away. Perhaps these get-togethers opened some doors and improved the work environment for women in state government a bit.

Perhaps one of the best things I did throughout my tenure as Ohio's First Lady was to always have a highly qualified and compassionate staff person coordinating and responding to constituency requests. Often, citizens came to me with requests after they had exhausted all other avenues in state government. They may already have written the governor, a department head, or their elected representative, and not gotten anywhere. In those instances, the First Lady became their last recourse. Sometimes we did find a way to persuade cabinet members to take another look at a person's issues, or at least show empathy. But especially when there was nothing that could be done to solve a citizen's problem, we still had an opportunity to show compassion and let them know that we were on their side.

Probably the most unconventional thing I did as First Lady was to take an interest in the budget process and vigorously campaign on tax issues. Both *Cleveland Magazine* and the *Plain Dealer* ferociously attacked me for voicing opinions on finances. One of the first things Dick had to do as governor was to raise the income tax. The previous governor let a surcharge tax expire just following our inauguration. To make matters worse, he used accounting procedures that were misleading. Basically, his budget that was supposed to last until summer was exhausted by the time Dick was sworn in. The only choice was to renew the temporary tax Governor Rhodes had imposed and significantly increase the income tax. The Republicans saw this as an opportunity to damage the new governor and put an issue on the ballot to repeal our renewal and increase. So the governor, his cabinet, I, and my staff had to hit the road again, as if the campaign had never stopped. Defending a tax increase must be the hardest campaign to wage, but without those increased resources we would not have been able to do anything worthwhile. In fact, we would not have been able to even continue the services that were in place.

One of the first attacks I sustained from the *Plain Dealer* was for being out in front on this issue. They seemed to think that it was unladylike and that I should stick to volunteering in hospitals or reading stories to children. To add insult to injury, they sent a woman reporter to do this premeditated hatchet job. She criticized my looks, the fact that I wasn't coloring my hair or wearing enough makeup; she ridiculed my supposed lack of interest in fashion. She questioned my character, my personality, my capacity for affection. She left no stone unturned—everything about me came under attack. The fact that I wanted to be active on public policy and budget issues was most violently criticized. With the banner headline "The Trouble with Dagmar," I became front-page news. But as soon as the story was out, the *Plain Dealer* received a barrage of letters to the editor from a most diverse crowd. Some of the writers were friends and supporters, but many were people I did not know. In many different ways they all basically said the same thing: Get off her back . . . Give her a chance . . . Why not let her do what she is capable of doing . . . We don't care if she looks or acts the part as long as she is interested in doing something that benefits Ohio. I was deeply grateful for the support. At events, strangers would come up and tell me how sorry they were about the *Plain Dealer* story. I told them that it came with the territory and that if they wanted to express their opinion, they should send a letter to the editor. "Send me a copy so I see it and can save and enjoy it in my old age," I told them. For weeks and weeks people did just that.

Finally the *Plain Dealer* sent one of its lieutenants to take me to lunch. The first thing out of this man's mouth was, "Well, you know, women should not be involved with economic issues." I just looked at him in disbelief. I reminded him that our director of taxation was a woman, as was our budget director. I then asked him if he meant "wives" not "women." He squirmed. I asked him if he was married and whether his wife was involved in their economic issues, their family budget.

"Well," he continued, "it's not so much that we at the *Plain Dealer* feel that way, but there are all kinds of people out there who think it unseemly for you to go on radio shows and television shows and talk about the budget." I told him that people are entitled to their opinions, certainly, but that there are plenty of other people who feel it's perfectly okay and, in fact, even admirable for the governor's wife to be well informed and able to talk about things that matter.

It became apparent that the real purpose for him taking me to lunch was to ask me to "call off" the letters to the editor. But since I hadn't organized them, I could not call them off. I told him that the *Plain Dealer* would have to live with it and print as many as appropriate for as long as they kept coming. He was not a happy man.

The media is every public person's greatest challenge. Dick and I learned to make a very clear distinction between the media and the *Plain Dealer,* however. The *Plain Dealer* was out to get the governor, and they tried to bring him down in as personal a way as possible. Anyone who was close to Dick was free game—whether they knew him personally, as in my case, or politically, as in the case of some cabinet members and constituency groups. The most uncalled-for attack was *PD* reporter Mary Ann Sharkey's attempt to "out" me

I never hid my support for gay-lesbian and bisexual civil rights. In fact Dick, who is also an adamant opponent of all discrimination, signed an executive order that for the first time prohibited discrimination in state government based on sexual preference. We should have included domestic partnership benefits, but at the time even the executive order seemed daring. As soon as our term was over, the Republicans rescinded the order. Both Dick and I supported the work of the gay-lesbian-bisexual community in educating the rest of Ohio. For the first time in Ohio's history, this group was offered the opportunity to exhibit at the state fair. Some fair officials objected, of course, but there was never any trouble from the public.

Furthermore, I remembered how my lesbian friends helped me the most in surviving the dual role of raising children while being politically active. Over the years, I have come to appreciate those women in a very special way, and I am most honored to have them as my friends. In many ways they have taken more time to be helpful than some of my straight female friends, who were preoccupied with raising their own families. When Stonewall Union in Cincinnati honored Dick and me with a joint award at their Annual Pride Banquet for simply treating the gay community with the same respect accorded other citizens in Ohio, and Dick could not go to the dinner, I went to accept the award for both of us. Upon our arrival, Marvin, my communication director, inquired if media was there and was informed that they weren't, which was misleading. While there was no mainstream media, the gay media was out in force.

I had prepared comments that included quotes from several authors, including Mother Teresa and Andrea Dworkin, to reflect my belief that all love was good. However, that intention was overlooked when I was quoted out of context in a gay publication. The Dworkin quote described the type of bonding that is shared between two women while making love, but in the article the quote was attributed to me, not Andrea. The author of the article, who was not at the dinner himself, made it sound like I was talking about my own personal experience with women as lovers and asserted that I all but came out at the dinner. I don't believe that the *Plain Dealer* had ever before or since used a gay publication as a source, but they used this unsubstantiated gossip and reprinted it as fact. I find it interesting that Dick was asked if I was a lesbian but I never was. That in itself shows that they were more interested in embarrassing him than in getting at the truth of the matter.

I choose not to use either "straight" or "gay" label. Over the years, I have allowed myself to fall in love with men and women. In order to call myself a lesbian, I would have to prefer making love to women. I don't. I only make love when in love. I have discovered that it is possible for some of us to fall in love across race, religion, nationality, and gender lines. I refer to people like me as philasexuals (as in Philadelphia, the city of brotherly love). A philasexual is someone who has to love the person s/he chooses to have sex with. While not always monogamous, philasexuals believe in the possibility and desirability of lifelong partnerships and friendships and support seeking the sacrament of marriage. Most important, we philasexuals can be trusted to keep our promises. Perhaps philasexuals are also easier prey for love addiction and co-dependence than most. And maybe female political spouses are more prone to co-dependence than nonpublic spouses.

. . .

Getting to know the spouses of the nation's governors was one of the perks of being First Lady of Ohio. From twenty-something to sixty-something, mostly female but also male, we were a diverse group indeed. Since we were of every imaginable political and personal persuasion, First Mates, as the men prefer to be called, could hardly be categorized. But the one thing we all had in common was a concern for protecting and promoting our spouse at almost any cost. Our political agenda was more often circumscribed by what seemed possible in our respective states than by personal preference. Every one of us was centrist rather than right or left wing. Every one of us had become an expert at synthesizing opposing viewpoints without compromising cherished values and significant constituencies. Whether feminist or born-again Christian or both, our politics were more a matter of the heart than a matter of ideological point of view. While limited by our personal feelings for our respective governors, we somehow felt free to honestly share with each other. As First Mates we did have enough influence to cross lines of power and could even move with impunity across patriarchal boundaries. Whereas the role of the governor is circumscribed by the constitution and the law, the governor's mate is bound only by convention and her imagination. Everything, though, depends on her relationship with the governor: if the marriage is solid and the friendship strong—and usually it is, otherwise they would be divorced or defeated—then working together is as simple as reading clues and complementing, rather than competing with, each other.

In our relationship, for instance, people would be somewhat taken aback by my willingness to confront and even contradict Dick in strategic planning sessions and behind-closed-doors political meetings. But I knew that Dick appreciated diversity of opinion and often publicly disagreed with me just to encourage others to show their doubts and disagreements so that he could then hammer out a solution to the challenge at hand. As a result, I acquired a reputation for being very outspoken and certainly intellectually independent from my spouse. But I would never have consciously worked against what I understood to be Dick's true feelings or the interests of what he supported. Most of us First Mates spend a good portion of our lives building and sustaining a political constituency, coupled with the fact that, at least in my generation, the female spouse was expected to raise the children, too. This created circumstances where, as political partners, we carried too heavy a load and were still expected to feel good about it—or at least pretend to. Sadly, most of us did just that and loved it more than was healthy for us or our children.

Still, when I think of the things Dick and I managed to do and the times we spent together doing them in politics and because of politics, I will always remember the eight years in the governor's office and living at the Residence as one of the most satisfying times of my life, second only to our years in India. Having acknowledged that, I do not want to deny the hardships we faced along the way. When First Ladies came together at the National Governors' Association winter and summer meetings, it was always a relief to be able to share some of this with each other.

One thing is certain: while in office it is difficult to find peers. First families are viewed as beyond reach, admired, envied, and sometimes reviled, but seldom included in real communal activities. Even among those in the governor's office, the cabinet, and the rest of the administration, the spouse, grown kids, siblings, parents, and other relatives are treated more as celebrities or unwelcome intrusions than as equal participants in a common cause. The spouse and family sessions at the National Governors' Association gave us a way to discuss those aspects of our lives and discover solutions to common challenges: how to run a governor's residence; how to decide what issues to support; how to project who we were and deflect media attacks on us and those we loved; how to continue professional interest to supplement often meager salaries; how to say no, and when to say yes; how to learn to market our own projects and ideas. While our spouses struggled to outshine each other in meetings that were designed to accomplish little, if anything, in order to protect the nonpartisan farce that kept the National Governors' Association staff happy and their jobs secure (many of them better paid than some of the governors), we mates met in less pretentious ways and managed to get to know each other well and support each others' struggles across party lines.

I was so unaware of the other spouses' party affiliations that I once made quite a fool of myself. After one of our Democratic conventions, I asked the First Lady of Rhode Island, "Why Pat, I really missed you at our convention; where were you?" Her bemused reply was, "Well, Dagmar, we don't go to Democratic conventions. Remember, I am a Republican." I was more surprised at myself than embarrassed. Under normal circumstances I am very political and quite partisan. But in this circle, while we all understood the value of partisan politics and respected the rules, what we needed from each other was insight into a shared adventure. Each of us believed that we had made it possible for good people to govern our respective states and that together we were shaping our destiny and that of our families and communities. This was a group of self-confident, very bright, and hardworking people. We were discreet, loyal, dependable, and very savvy. Many of us did get caught in media controversies, but most of us also learned not only how to avoid the worst but how to make the best of even the worst possible interpretation of our true intentions.

Once a year we would come together in a governor's spouse seminar. During her tenure as First Lady of the NGA, Kitty Dukakis was the first to invite us all to the Kennedy School of Public Policy. And in our last year in office I was grateful to Dr. Elizabeth Gee, the wife of the president of Ohio State University, and Dr. Astrid Mergit, a faculty member in the school of public policy at OSU, for organizing a most substantive and enjoyable seminar for spouses of the NGA members. The highlight of these get-togethers was always the pajama party. Male and female First Mates came together in the largest suite of the hotel in our robes and pajamas, and over drinks and munchies we let go and shared some of our most private feelings and fears. Over the years, we also began seeing some men enter the network. Arthur Kunin, a physician and First Mate of Vermont, was the first male participant at the traditional pajama party. The first time Arthur came into the NGA meeting, he gave us lecture on osteoporosis and persuaded those of us in the throes of premenopause to eat large quantities of Tums in order to prevent calcium deficiencies. In some ways, being First Mate was easier for the men than for the women, as they usually had a clear-cut profession and career separate from their governor spouse; nor were they expected to play hostess and/or social worker to the whole state. Also, they were seldom fully responsible for the care and upbringing of the First Family's children.

I remember these gatherings were as good as some of the best consciousness-raising sessions at the height of the women's movement. I recall vividly when we discovered that the governor of Kansas had chosen to announce his plan to divorce his spouse the very weekend she was out of the state at our seminar. We all closed ranks and tried to console and support her as best we could. That night all of us had personal horror tales of staff members attempting to outmaneuver family and friends and shared concerns about the danger of isolation in office. A few years later Paula Blanchard had done all the work for one of our sessions but was no longer First Lady by the time we arrived in Michigan. In her case, the divorce seemed to be less traumatic and more by mutual agreement, but still we felt saddened by the situation and the fact that we had to sneak her into our suite behind her own governor's back.

We First Mates shared many good ideas. Something that worked in one state presumably could work in other states. We would present successful projects to one another along with thoughts as to how we made them work. I came to accept that each of us had to invent our own role based on our personal relationship with our spouse, the specific political realities of our respective states, and our own preferences and talents. Probably half of the First Mates chose to stay in the background, and about a quarter were moderately active with a project here or there. Only about 10 percent were as active as I was, and most of us probably did what our spouses wanted us to do. There were as many different ways of being First Mate as there were of being governor. At these meetings we talked a lot about the difficulties in keeping our relationships with our spouses healthy, but we felt uncomfortable being too honest about the nature of the difficulties we were facing. As usual, I was more outspoken than most. I acknowledged that affairs do happen and that to me the most important thing in any relationship is honesty. (Little did I know then that my own spouse was not as honest as I thought. But back then I had no insight into the depth of my own codependence on marriage and would surely have vehemently denied my own dysfunction.) While we spouses tried hard to be open and honest with each other, many of our governors were plotting and planning to become president, so there was always the possibility that someday we might have to battle each other in a political campaign. Kitty Dukakis and Hillary Clinton were certainly in that position at the time I was First Lady. While we shared much, to be sure, we also kept much heartache hidden.

Over time the summer NGA meetings came to focus on the life of the family, and our children were included so that they could meet other kids in the same personal/political predicament. At their first meeting, the Celeste kids formed a children's forum where their peers could get together and talk about what it was like to be the child of a governor. Also, at family breakfasts one family would present the pros and cons of living the life of a First Family. The pros included invitations to ski outings, interesting vacations, NGA events, fancy affairs; the cons included parental absences and a rushed, fragmented family life. I have come to realize that the prime dangers of this life in a fish bowl are holding back, denial, and emotional dishonesty.

Another con was the itinerant nature of many political families.

When we bought Himmelblau House on Kelley's Island, we had been homeless for years. The original homestead on Lake Avenue had to be sold to finance college educations for the kids. Luxurious as the Residence was, the salary of the sixty-fourth governor was less than that of his own health director. With six children—three in college and three at home—making ends meet was not just a public budget challenge for Dick. I remember him sitting and wondering whose bill to pay, no doubt feeling frustrated and frantic. An honest politician may become respected, but, more likely, s/he'll go broke first.

On balance, the benefits of public life far outweighed the disadvantages, and I would not trade those years for any amount of money or comfort. I am grateful to have spent the best years our lives together raising children and raising hell, and I am proud of the work Dick and I did together. Together, we and the many Celestials made Ohio just a little better, and to this day I meet folks almost daily who remember and agree.

I've come to see those days as First Lady of Ohio as some of the brightest pieces in my life's quilt, with all its passion and richly varied, complex, and contradictory pattern. Despite its sometimes awkwardness and even oppressiveness, it's still dazzlingly creative and beautiful. I continue to add fresh shapes, colors, and textures to our quilt and to our personal and political partnership.

Postscript

August 24, 1999

Unless the Lord builds the house, its builders labor in vain.
—Psalm 127:1

Sometime this summer, I received an invitation to join First Lady Hope Taft in building Habitat for Humanity's House of Hope in Canton. This request had a certain serendipity and synergy for me.

Ever since I began receiving alimony payments, I have contributed a small but symbolically significant monthly amount to Habitat, Dick's favorite charity. When we met the organizations's founder couple at a dinner during our first Renaissance Weekend, Dick and I both wanted to participate in this grace-filled opus of reconciliation. Most everyone knows by now that Habitat builds homes for poor people around the world, but what few people realize is that the call to do this work originated in the founders' willingness to choose reconciliation over divorce. So I felt disappointed and puzzled when Dick began to volunteer alone and never once invited me to join him. To make matters worse, during a Habitat building tour in Africa, he claimed to have experienced a spiritual awakening that eventually led to his leaving our marriage.

My enthusiasm for "the theology of the hammer" was thereafter understandably weakened, and my confusion about how to best read and follow God's will increased. I tried to be understanding about Dick's desire for breathing space but also became more and more resentful of Habitat's role in our life. As he rose in the leadership ranks of that organization, his commitment to maintaining and rebuilding our relationship waned. Sadly, the last present I ever received from my husband was a ceramic cookie jar in the shape of a Habitat House to commemorate a thousand-dollar contribution he gave in my name to build the first Habitat Women's House in Columbus.

During a family intervention, I came to realize the extent of our problems and discovered that besides the past affairs I had been aware of, there were women all over the country, many of whom were expecting to take my place.

In one of our many marriage encounter dialogues, he once wrote to me that the five characteristics he loved most about me were my spirituality, my intellectual tenacity, my honesty, my loyalty, and my compassion: "You work the boundaries—explore and push out. I work the center—invent and pull in. I am spiritually sensitive, intellectually curious; you are spiritually vigorous and intellectually disciplined. I am tolerant of faults; you are outspoken and critical. I am a good mediator; you are a valiant mentor. And both of us are caring parents." I believed this to be an accurate assessment of our strengths and weaknesses but saw it as a healthy, synergistic polarity between us and as complimentary rather than contradictory. But we were both too sick to hear the deepest longing in the other's voice . . . or even in our own hearts.

Dick and I did not understand the difference between nostalgia and history, nor did we know the exchange rate between danger and pleasure. We simply became more and more estranged in our desire to labor on the fiction called "our" home and "our" world. A Habitat standard says that whenever we come together to build, someone will sooner or later tell us that when that big hurricane hit, none of the Habitat homes blew apart simply because they had more nails in them than did any other home due to the many mistakes made by novice builders. When Dick and I met, we were not only novices but were fearless to the point of peril and simply assumed that we could continue to keep the wolf at bay by using more nails to build a stonger home.

• • •

Swing low so I
can step inside—
a humming ship of voices
big with all

the wrongs done
done them.
No sound this generous
could fail:

ride joy until
it cracks like an egg,
make sorrow
seethe and whisper. . . .
                    —Rita Dove, "Gospel"

Considering my mixed history with Habitat, it took some soul-searching before I accepted Hope Taft's invitation to bring some friends and lend a hand. But I did go, and I had fun and learned quite a bit about what not to do with a hammer.

When, two months later, the invitation came to help welcome Marlene and Mikaila into their new home and to celebrate the completion and dedication of the house I'd helped build, I wasn't surprised—only amused—that it should correspond with our thirty-seventh wedding anniversary. At the dedication, Hope Taft spoke about the Shaker belief of "hands to heart and heart to God" and how grateful she was to each and every one of us for our help in building a new foundation, special windows of opportunity, and the doors to a new future not only for Marlene and her daughter but for ourselves and our own dreams of new beginnings. She then presented Mikaila with a special gift: sanded, polished play blocks made from the wood scraps used in the building of the house.

Memories of better times came rushing in. Of times when our kids were young enough to enjoy building with blocks, times when we were in love enough to believe we could overcome anything, times when I was centered *enough to move in and out of people's lives gracing celebrations, educating, building, organizing, and empowering our growing constituency for change with conscience.*

When I joined in the singing of the final song of this moving dedication ceremony, I realized we were singing the old folk ballad Dick and I used to croon to each other.

The river is wide I cannot cross over
And neither have I wings to fly
Build me a boat that can carry two
And both shall row my love and I.

Oh love is handsome and love is fine
Gay as a jewel when first it's new
But love grows old and waxes cold
And fades away like morning dew.

A ship there is and she sails the seas
She's laden deep as deep can be
But not so deep as the love I'm in
And I know not if I sink or swim.

As we were leaving, Marlene asked us to put some thought, prayer, or just our name into the freshly whitewashed entryway closet. I was tempted to put "Solo Dios basta," the Carmelite version of Ohio's state motto, "With God all things are possible," but I realized that simply "Dagmar" would do.

Index

compiled by Nancy Birk

"We Can Do Together"

was designed and composed by Christine Brooks

in 10/14 Plantin Light with display text in Wembley Light;

on a Macintosh G4 using PageMaker 6.5;

printed on 55# Supple Opaque stock

by Thomson-Shore, Inc., of Dexter, Michigan;

and published by

THE KENT STATE UNIVERSITY PRESS

Kent, Ohio 44242